3064
4727

FAMOUS AIRCRAFT:

THE AT-6 HARVARD

by

Len Morgan

Scale drawings: Richard Groh

A Len Morgan Book

ARCO PUBLISHING CO., INC.
219 Park Avenue South
New York, N.Y. 10003

COVER DRAWING:

RCAF Harvard II of No. 14 Service Flying Training School, Aylmer, Ontario.

ACKNOWLEDGEMENT

A number of individuals and organizations assisted in the preparation of this book. My thanks to G. M. Cameron, David Menard, Margaret Morgan, Terry Morgan, Bill Daniels, Robert O'Hara, Jose R. de Mendonca, Canadian Car and Foundry Company, North American Aviation, The Roundel, and the U.S. Forest Service. A very special word of thanks to Arnold Nagtegaal who made his entire collection of AT-6 Harvard photographs available for use in this book. — L. M.

Second printing, June 1966

Library of Congress catalog card number 65-26763
Arco catalog number 1413

Manufactured in the United States of America

THE FAMOUS AIRCRAFT SERIES

The P-51 Mustang
The P-47 Thunderbolt
The Planes the Aces Flew
LZ 129 Hindenburg
The Douglas DC-3
The Seaplanes
The B-17 Flying Fortress
The F-86 Sabre
The AT-6 Harvard
The Lockheed Constellation (in preparation)
The B-58 Hustler (in preparation)
The Boeing 707 (in preparation)
The Messerschmitt Me. 109 (in preparation)
The P-38 Lightning (in preparation)

The Royal California Air Force

A blue truck drove along a country road in Ontario on a summer morning in 1941. In back, on wood seats under the canvas top, a dozen boys of college age faced each other over a pile of black kit bags. They wore blue uniforms and made a great deal of noise laughing and telling jokes. They shouted and waved at two pretty girls in a car who trailed the truck for a mile before speeding past with a taunting blare of their horn. The leisurely progress of the truck and the lighthearted mood of its riders told little of the real purpose of the trip. This was for each of them the realization of a lifelong dream; the horseplay was an effort to disguise excitement.

The truck turned from the main road and ran along a narrow lane leading to a gate over which hung a sign, "No. 9 Elementary Flying Training School." It stopped and the driver spoke to the guard.

"Another load of Americans come to save us from the Nazis."

"Winston will be relieved. I'll call him right away."

The truck drove through the gate and into the small camp that lay beyond, pulling up before a wood barracks. A short, red-faced British sergeant who had somehow found himself in this remote corner of the Empire waited for the noisy riders to climb down. Noticing him, they arranged themselves in a rough line. The sergeant regarded this pitiful effort with an expression of utter disdain. The nervous shuffling of feet settled into an uncomfortable silence. Finally the sergeant spoke to himself, quietly.

"My bloody nerves." He shook his head the way people do at funerals.

He walked slowly around his new charges, hands clasped behind him, peering into every face. He paused at the end of the ragged line to sight along the uneven row of heads. What he saw made him close his eyes and shudder. Controlling himself with visible effort he suddenly strode to the front of the group and bawled, "Tennnnnnnnn - shun!" An uneasy minute passed before he spoke.

"If *this* is what His Majesty's air force has come to, God help us." Strolling along the line he looked through each boy.

"Oh, well, we'll have to make the best of it, I suppose. My name is Flight Sergeant Maxwell and you chaps are going to get to know me very well indeed during your stay here. Yes, very well indeed." He paused for emphasis.

"I know you're here to learn to handle these bloomin' aeroplanes and all that but first you're bloody well going to learn how to march and make no mistake about it." He regarded the recruits with fresh distaste. "You look like a lot of sloppy Navy people! Well, this isn't the Navy. This is the Royal Canadian Air Force, and we expect much more than the Navy. Is that quite clear?" He searched the expressionless faces as if expecting a reply. Receiving none, he pulled a paper from his pocket.

"All right then, answer to your names. Woods?"

"Here."

"Baldwin?"

"Here."

"Vogel?"

"Here."

"Morgan?"

"Here."

Woods . . . Baldwin . . . Vogel . . . the young faces look out from the fading picture by my desk. And there's Teagarden and Mudge and Wynne. And those two were Wendt and Sanders. I can remember the sergeant saying that first day, "Vogel? Wendt? Are you lads sure you're reporting to the right station?"

We laughed and this pleased him for he imagined himself to be — and indeed he was — a man with a genuine sense of humor. Old Bloody Nerves was all right and we knew it that moment. He was no one's fool, mind you, but a fair man and all that a good disciplinarian should be.

The faces . . . there's Hallihan. And Rushton. And that fellow was Stafford from Ohio, or was it New York? How well I remember them and the day we arrived at St. Catherines. Yet, as the years roll by, it seems increasingly more of an illusion than a real bit of personal history. Oh, it all happened, I know; these old pictures, the RCAF logbook and the strange blue uniform packed away in the attic prove it. And the phone call I get at intervals that always begins, "How's my old "C" Flight buddy?" Yes, it all happened, even if I now have to turn the pictures over sometimes to match the names and faces. How long ago is twenty-four years anyway?

The clumsy scene we played before Sergeant Maxwell that day had its bizarre twist even though it was being repeated then at training fields throughout Canada. We were Americans, citizens of a nation at peace, enlisted in the service of a nation at war. Citizens, I said, for we were never asked to swear allegiance to the King. We signed agreements to serve "for the duration and a period of demobilization of up to one year," contracts from which we were immediately released when the chance came later in the war to join our own country's forces. About eight thousand Americans took this quicker way into the air. These circumstances were by no means precedent-setting. The Eagle Squadrons were organized in the pattern of the Lafayette Escadrille of World War I fame. Our own training experiences were described in detail many years earlier by Elliott White Springs, an American who flew with Billy Bishop. Only the dates changed.

We were there for many reasons — we were too young for the peacetime Air Corps, or too old, or did not have the required two-college years — or something. We were there for one reason, to learn to fly. None of us, at that stage, had strong feelings about the war.

The assembled members of "Course 32" on the parade ground at No. 9 Elementary Flying Training School, July, 1941. Washouts and ground school failures were to cut this group almost in half.

Our dozen was joined at No. 9 by a truckload of Canadians, two Australians and some Englishmen who did have strong feelings about the war. Each new load of arrivals was promptly dressed down by Sergeant Maxwell and sent off to wax the barracks floor, his favorite punishment. There are forty-one of us in the group picture made two Sundays later and there is actually a military look about us.

The class was nearly a third American and the sign over the main gate was altered one night to read, "Royal California Air Force," a stupid stunt that cost us, including the puzzled English, two hours of extra drill.

"California? Where's this California, Rodney?" one asked.

"One of the islands we own in the Pacific, old boy, somewhere near Pitcairn, I'd say."

"Of course, one of the colonies."

"Why else would all of these strange California people be joining us to overthrow the Hun? Frightfully decent of them, wouldn't you say?"

It was a Duke's Mixture and the mixing produced surprising results, one being the discovery that the Australians, when we eventually learned what they were saying, proved themselves superior braggards to the Texans. We had all completed several weeks of ITS (Initial Training School), a brief but intensive course to weed out applicants with insufficient math for navigation. At ITS we also learned to handle the Springfield rifle. Not to shoot it, you understand, but to clean it and march with it. The staff at No. 9 soon put us to work. The class was split into two groups, one of which attended ground-school while the other flew. If you flew in the morning you took signals, nav, aero engines, parachutes, instruments and other studies in the afternoon. We worked hard in both phases.

No one will ever do a book on the Fleet, which is the elementary trainer we flew at St. Kitts. And it is a shame for it was in its own way, and to those of us who flew it, as wonderful and exciting as the Mustang or Spitfire. You always feel this way about the first plane you fly even when you have graduated to better things and realize what a slow clunker it was. You never lose that initial affection or forget the first aerial thrills it provided.

Elementary flight training in Canada then utilized the famous deHavilland Tiger Moth and the Fleet Finch. Both types are now referred to as "antiques" by those who restore old aircraft and this does not make me feel like a young man. The Moth had a slender fuselage, swept wings and sat close to the ground on two fat little tires. Its dainty appearance belied a robust constitution. The Fleet looked as rugged as it was. A four cylinder, air-cooled Gipsy Major powered the Moth while a Kinner five-cylinder radial hung in the Fleet. Both ships did the job as well as any other primary trainers of the day.

The Moth and Fleet approximated in size, general appearance and performance the fighter aircraft of the first air war. Our grass field with its single hangar and row of small biplanes was almost a copy of a 1918 aerodome in France, except that the Fleets were all painted bright yellow. This obvious similarity was not lost on boys who had for years devoured yarns about Spads and Nieuports. As soon as the barracks floor had been waxed to the satisfaction of Old Bloody Nerves, we went down to the hangar to watch the upper classmen fly.

The famous Tiger Moth. More than 9,000 of these stout little elementary trainers were built during a fourteen-year production life. Moths replaced the Fleets at No. 9 Elementary Flying Training School during March, 1942. (Photo: Canadian Department of National Defense)

Pilot descends from Fleet Finch at No. 7 Elementary Flying Training School, Windsor, 22 July 1940. (Photo: Canadian Department of National Defense)

Our instructors were civilians, Canadian and American. I drew Mr. Al Bennett, or he drew me, depending upon how you see it. He was a quiet, inoffensive fellow, anything but the shouting, abusive bully who too often found (and still finds) his way into this line of work. A quick walkaround of Fleet Number 4568 satisfied him that his new student knew the difference between rudder and elevator. He showed me how to adjust my parachute, the quick-release type used by all British flying services with a mechanism by which all straps could be undone with a single smash of the fist. This can be important if you have to bail out over water. Fleet students rode in the front seat, dual or solo, except for instrument training.

Thirty minutes later we were pounding along at 3,000 feet with the Kinner in my lap making a terrific racket. When Mr. Bennett banked the ship I looked between the wings and wondered why we did not slip right into the farms below, a typical first reaction. Leveling out, he spoke through the Gosport tube, "All right, Morgan, you have control." I grabbed the stick and left my fingerprints there for all time.

"Relax, son, relax. It won't bite you. Fly it with two fingers — and don't stand on the rudders."

I sat back down on my chute and tried to do it his way. We stumbled through the Ontario sky like a sick buzzard but I had control! Whatever crude path we cut through space was mine. It was me making that rattling old Kinner bob on the horizon, me pulling up that low wing, me slamming us both in our seats — and if you have never learned to fly you will never really understand how it felt.

Lindbergh sweating his fuel over the dark Atlantic had never worked like this or perspired as freely. I would never master this weaving machine with a mind of its own. After just the right amount of this (he was a born instructor if one ever lived) I heard in my helmet, "Okay, I have control," and the ship settled instantly into normal flight. He flew us home and I marvelled at his skill as we dropped from the sky, shot across the fence at enormous speed and kissed the earth with an audible swish of rubber through grass. The first flight was over and I was exhausted, somewhat discouraged and absolutely determined to learn how it was done.

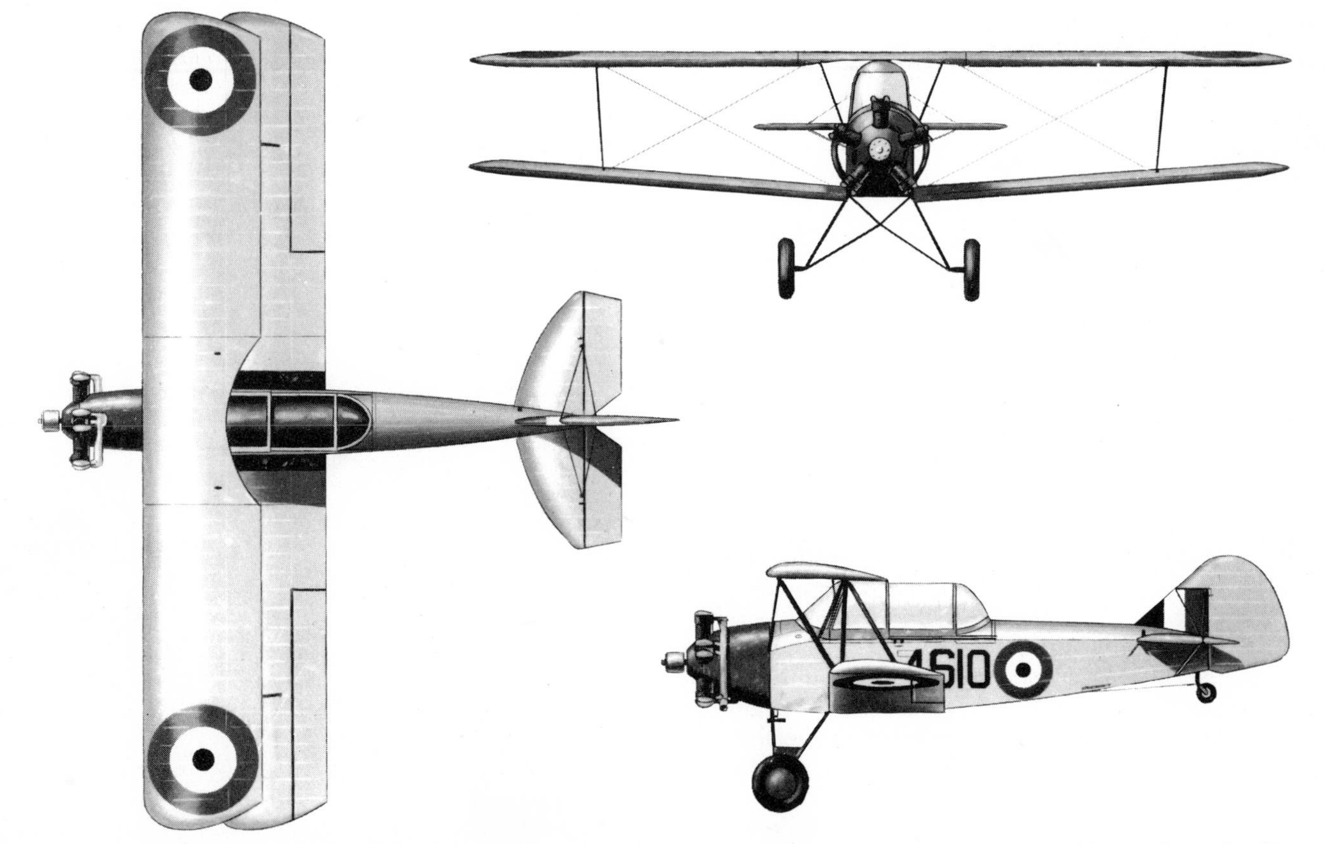

Fleet Finch primary trainer of No. 9 Elementary Flying Training School. This ship, No. 4610, was flown by the author on his first solo trip. The Fleet was powered by the very reliable Kinner B-5 five-cylinder radial. Maximum speed was 113 miles per hour. Span and length were 28 ft. and 21 ft., 8 in., respectively.

Typical RCAF student during early days of World War II used seat-pack type parachute with quick-release button.

"Let's get a coke and try it again," said Mr. Bennett.

Ten days later he said, "Make one more circuit and landing just like the last one, but drop me off at the hangar first." The first solo, just like that. On the downwind leg I twisted twice to look into the empty back seat and laughed loud enough to hear myself above the Kinner's roar. When I walked into the hangar a few minutes later, Mr. Bennett was trying hard to look relaxed. Someone asked him if he usually smoked two cigarettes at once. Then I bought him a coke.

My logbook shows sixty-five hours and fifty minutes flown at St. Kitts. Our class dwindled to twenty-two during those six short weeks. Washouts and groundschool failures got nineteen. There was Meatball Pedlar (I don't know why we called him that) whose engine quit as he came out of a right hand spin. Forgetting the restarting procedure and in spite of the fact he was right over the field, Meatball picked a small clear spot on the far side of town, glided all the way there on the ragged edge of a stall and squeezed into a field so small they couldn't fly it out. He didn't scratch it. He got by with this but the navigation final got him.

And there was the fellow who wouldn't land. Thirty or more times he made the circuit, executed a beautiful approach and then crammed everything to the firewall just before touchdown. They grounded the rest of us while an instructor flew alongside him, trying to lead him to earth. It didn't work. Finally, just at dusk, the frightened boy dropped onto the grass in a perfect three-point. The next day he was on his way to gunner's school.

And the English boy who dropped in so hard he wrote off his ship. I saw it happen. He must have fallen thirty feet, in a full stall. The Fleet hit on all three wheels but it couldn't take this. The fuselage bent in the middle, the wings sagged, the gear crumpled. Out of the cloud of dust the Fleet staggered on flat tires, wires trailing under the broken tail, smashed prop beating the ground. The student taxied to the line, swung around and parked neatly between two intact trainers, stiff upper lip to the end. He became a navigator.

Another fellow did a fine job until his solo. He circled the field once, landed nicely, taxied in, shut down and went to see the C. O. "Sir, I don't want to be a pilot," he said, and this was what he meant. It was just not what he thought it would be and he felt he would never be any good at it. He wanted to serve in any flying capacity except as a pilot. He was transferred to navigator's school and he doubtless made a good one.

At. St. Kitts we learned the fundamentals of navigation, engines, meteorology and related subjects — and a little bit about flying. We smashed our fair share of wingtips, shattered a few props and wrote off one airplane completely. On August 16 we packed our kit bags, shook hands with our instructors and climbed aboard trucks. Not one of us failed to seek out Old Bloody Nerves.

"Thanks again, Sarge, for getting me off the hook with the Old Man."

"Very good, lad, and mind that it doesn't happen again." Then, marching importantly around us, "What is this, a bloomin' tea party? You're slopping about like a lot of Navy people! Into the lorries, come along. My bloody nerves!"

We rode through the gate and read for the last time the sign that hung above it. Not one of us had been hurt; not one of us had been killed. We had maintained the perfect safety record at St. Kitts, the record Old Bloody Nerves was so proud of. No one said much as we turned off the narrow lane onto the main road and lost sight of him standing under the sign.

May the grass grow green where once we flew the Fleet.

Finch Trainers of No. 7 EFTS, Windsor. (Photo: Canadian Department of National Defense)

Who Jumped American Airlines?

Such was the level of training and experience of an RCAF flying student when he was introduced to the Harvard during World War II. Additional back-ground instruction would certainly have been desirable but the record indicates it was not essential. The fatality rate among Harvard students was amazingly low in Canada, in fact it was lower than that accepted in some other air forces which gave their cadets as much as a year's training prior to advanced flight instruction. The reason for this, I think, is that the Canadians concentrated on fundamentals whereas there was a tendency in other Allied services to expose students to all aspects of military flying. The purpose was of course to produce a well-rounded graduate, but there is such a thing as teaching too much too fast. Learning to fly an airplane as potent as the Harvard was demanding enough in itself, without any extra pressures.

This personal comment is open to argument. As an RCAF-trained pilot I am prone to defend the system that taught me. My flying friends who were trained in the Army and Navy tell me they were repeatedly reminded that their instruction was the best in the world, and that this made them the best in the world. Perhaps this is the best psychology to use on a young pilot trainee; perhaps it serves to instill him with confidence.

The Canadian approach was quite different. We were quietly reminded from time to time that while our training was second to none, we were still embryo pilots — that's the exact term used by one officer — with plenty left to learn. We were also reminded that the Germans knew a thing or two about flying, not that we could not match them if we paid close attention to our more experienced superiors. A Battle of Britain ace who spoke to us on the troopship put it this way, "Six months from today half of you fighter chaps will be dead. That's right, I said dead. Those of you who die will not die because you haven't received adequate training but because you didn't listen to your flight leaders. I lost most of my friends last year for this very stupid reason. Learn to eat, sleep and breathe fighter flying; follow exactly the instructions you are given and you'll not only survive, you may get a Jerry or two in the bargain. Fighter pilots die for good reasons, and they are usually needless reasons."

The American members of "C" Flight after receiving their wings at No. 14 Service Flying Training School on 21 November 1941. (White flash in cap denotes an aircrew trainee; propellor on sleeve indicates rank of Leading Aircraftsman, the rating of all RCAF student airmen). Georgia, Kentucky, Alabama, Connecticut, Colorado, Texas, Minnesota, Pennsylvania and New York are represented here.

The rugged, faithful old Anson on which most of the RAF's bomber crews of World War II received their first multi-engine training. Harvard pilots called it, "ten thousand aircraft parts flying in close formation". (Photo: Canadian Department of National Defense)

The surviving twenty-two members of our St. Kitts class were split into two groups, half going to multi-engine training in Ansons, the rest of us to Harvards. My crowd reported to No. 14 Service Flying Training School at Aylmer, Ontario, where we were joined by graduates from several other EFTSs — Canadians, Americans, Englishmen and a sprinkling of Australians and New Zealanders. We were divided into units, ours — thirteen Americans and fourteen Canadians — becoming "C" Flight. After unloading our baggage we took a look around the new base.

Where civilian-operated St. Kitts had been a quiet little grass field with one small hangar and a row of wood barracks, Aylmer boasted a long line of steel hangars, concrete runways and a sprawling camp area. The place was strictly air force and all business. It was outfitted with Harvard IIs, some built in the United States and some under license at Noorduyn's Montreal plant. "Harvard" is the popular name we used, that is, and which was employed throughout the British flying services. The ship was of course the famous North American-designed AT-6, known in Navy circles as the SNJ. The American popular name was supposed to be "Texan," but it never caught on anymore than "Skytrain" replaced C-47 or "Commando" replaced C-46. "Texan" was something you saw in books; to Army pilots it was invariably the "AT-6."

Our particular ships incorporated a few British modifications such as the circular stick grip used on English fighters and the big, round floor-mounted compass that appeared to have been taken from a battleship. These were nickle-and-dime items making no real difference in

RCAF Harvard IIA. The first fifteen Canadian Harvard Is were obtained from North American Aviation shortly before World War II. Ninety additional IIAs were ordered in 1940. In order to preserve U. S. neutrality, all ninety aircraft had to be flown to the international boundary, then pushed or pulled to the Canadian side! Canadian pilots then picked up the ships and flew them to their ultimate destinations. (Photo: North American Aviation)

the plane's appearance or performance.

We walked into "C" Flight's hangar and inspected a Harvard at close range. It was a huge, all-metal creation with a tremendous 600 horsepower Pratt and Whitney nine-cylinder radial glistening darkly under an enormous cowl. It was obviously put together like a brick outhouse. The Harvard rested on a rather narrow gear which folded inward in flight. After the simple cloth-covered Fleet, the Harvard looked massive, rugged, heavy, complex. There was a feeling of brute strength about it. Climbing up on the left wing we peered into the open front cockpit and caught our breath. The wide spaces on each side of the aluminum seat were crammed with handles, wheels and levers of all shapes, sizes and mysterious uses. The broad instrument panel contained a hopeless confusion of black-faced dials and toggle switches. More handles protruded from beneath the instruments and between the big rudder pedals.

"Hey, look at the numbers on the A. S. I."

"Man, it reads 300 on the top side!"

"There's that sensitive altimeter they talked about."

"Are we supposed to watch all of this junk and fly at the same time?"

American military schools of this era led the flying student gradually through primary training in Stearmans to basic school in the Vultee Vibrator and finally to the big, powerful AT-6. By the time a cadet stepped into his first AT-6 he was a reasonably accomplished pilot.

Originators of the British Commonwealth Air Training Plan elected to bypass the intermediate (basic) stage and move the 65-hour student from Fleet or Moth school right into the final stage of training. Some Canadian and American training experts, watching this plan take shape, were dubious. It was too fast, they argued. A sixty-hour pupil couldn't handle 600 horsepower.

Looking back we can see that the BCATP was sound. The AT-6 was eventually to become the USAF's primary trainer, the first plane a recruit flew! At the time the question was a serious one. The Canadians were, as it turned out, a step ahead of Americans on this point.

Sergeant Bob Campbell, a pleasant and likeable fellow of 700 hours experience, was my new instructor. He took me for a thirty minute familiarization hop on the first training day and I immediately fell in love with the big Harvard. I rode in the back seat as we barrelled merrily across the countryside under a low ceiling, tearing into turns that pinned me to my chute. I observed the wild instrument readings with amazement, listened carefully to his running description of the ship's operation and watched the trees streak by beneath the large metal wing. It was a tremendous experience. We raced for the field in heavy rain, touched down on the wet concrete at an impossible velocity and somehow stopped before we ran out of airport. I did not need to be told that I hadn't learned much in the Fleet.

The remainder of the afternoon was spent in a hangared Harvard learning the tarmac check and pre-takeoff drill. H-T-M-P-C-G-T for hydraulics, trim, mixture, pitch, carburetor heat, gas and throttle — and I didn't need my log to remember that. H-T-M-P-C-G-T, over and over and over until we said it in our sleep.

The next morning I rode up front and poor Sergeant Campbell, strapped in the rear, started teaching me how to handle this monster. Never to this day have I envied the Harvard instructor. He had almost no forward vision when the tail was down, and that's when the ship was at its meanest — during ground roll after landing. While the Harvard was a relatively easy ship to fly, it had a narrow gear and a high center of gravity. When the tail dropped on landing the wing blanketed out the tail group, rendering the rudder to a large degree ineffective. This unfortunate combination (also possessed by the Navy's Wildcat) made crosswind landings more than a little interesting. On the early Harvards which we flew, the rudder pedals were tied to the tailwheel — up to a point, that is. A sharp kick of either rudder would disengage the tailwheel, allowing the ship to swing around in its own length. This was a necessary feature for parking the ship in close quarters. On the runway it often worked against the pilot, however. You'd touch down in a cross wind and the nose would swing as the ship attempted to weathercock; you'd counter with rudder to straighten out. Jab it a hair to much and the tailwheel would come loose with a sickening snap. From this point onward things happened fast, unless you were quick with the brakes. The idea was to apply a few degrees of corrective rudder and hold it until heading was under control. No quick, deep kicks. Most of this we learned the hard way.

The next afternoon a French-Canadian of our flight had his tailwheel break loose and he got a wingtip and landing gear stuck in the ensuing crazy ride off the runway. The next day it was my turn. Landing after a dual period the nose swung left. I hit the rudder hard and almost immediately felt the tailwheel come unglued. Campbell grabbed it but we were already off to the races. Around we rushed in a slewing one-wheel turn, one wingtip pointing at the sky, the other dragging through the grass alongside the runway. I thought we would never stop. Finally we slumped back onto all three wheels, facing across the runway, engine still ticking over. We had turned 450 degrees during the mad ride. I taxied in feeling like an utter fool. The fact that everyone else was doing it didn't help. The mechanics came out, pulled grass from the wingtip light and pronounced the ship intact. I breathed again. Sergeant Campbell said let's call it a day.

An hour later, with another American on the stick, it happened all over again. This time they taxied in with a smashed wingtip. Poor Sergeant Campbell.

After four hours of dual, I was sent up with the officer commanding our flight. He kept me in the circuit thirty minutes, chewed me out as I'd never been chewed before — and I had it coming — then signed my solo permit. Then I flew the howling monster alone for the first time or, to be more honest about it, I hung on tight while it took me for a wild ride through the sky. Somehow I got the thing back to "C" Flight's hangar unscratched.

The days flew by and we learned to think faster, to react instinctively, to glance at the big panel and learn what it had to tell, to judge, to estimate, to work on two problems at the same time and find the right answer to each, to anticipate trouble before it happened, to meet emergencies calmly, to extracate ourselves from hairy situations, to behave a little more like professional air-

Too much for a sixty-hour student? (Photo: North American Aviation)

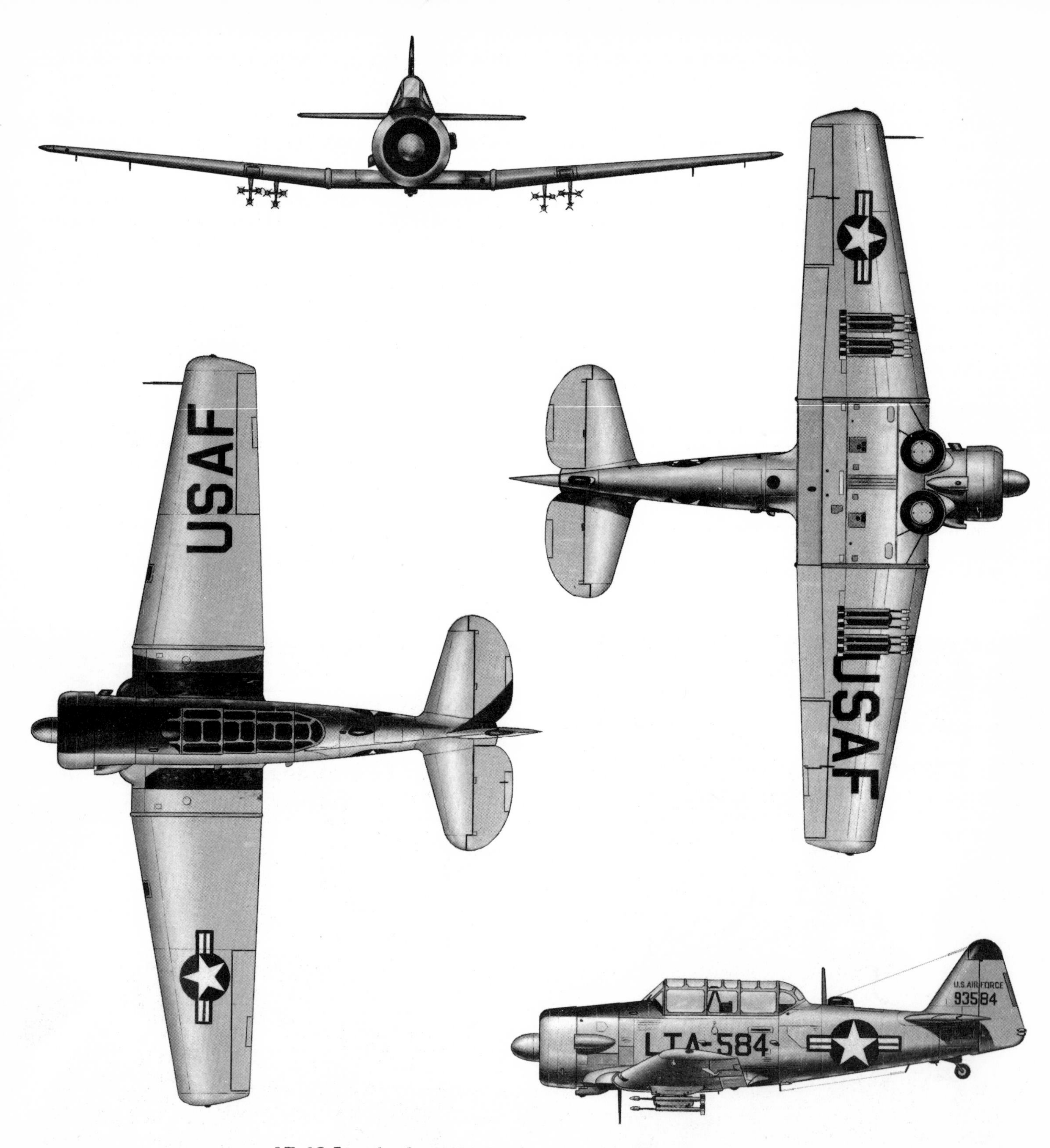

LT-6G flown by the 6147th Tactical Control Group, Korea, 1952.

During the Korean War, T-6s of the 6147th were employed as spotter planes for fighter-bombers. Their mission was to seek out concealed or other targets which were difficult to spot from the faster-moving jets. "When the planes with the bombs and rockets showed up", reported Lieutenant General Lauris Norstad after a tour of the front, "the T-6s more often than not led them to the attack to make sure they'd hit the right things. They would go right down and blow the leaves off the targets so the pilots behind them could see what they were supposed to blast".

men. We were green, we were awkward, we were right part of the time and scared most of the time — but we were learning.

The rivalry between flights was keen. We delighted in the published news that "F" Flight had racked up $20,000 worth of aircraft damage while "C" Flight had chalked up the lowest total. We were sobered by the news that two students in an "E" Flight Harvard, graduates of another EFTS, had spun in a few miles away. We were saddened to learn that a Georgia boy had flown a St. Kitts Fleet into high tension lines and incinerated himself while his mother and instructor watched.

The Harvard was no Saturday afternoon toy; it was capable of getting even an experienced pilot into real trouble. I learned this while doing a few weeks of guard duty at Trenton pending assignment to ITS. An officer with combat fighter time under his belt spun in near the base for no apparent reason. The yellow Harvard hit flat and level, so that the fuselage was wrenched from its mounts and rested lengthwise along the wing. The pilot had jumped too late. I can see the reddened, grotesquely crumpled form as it lay where it hit, a few inches ahead of the muddy engine.

Trouble with a happier ending befell one of the Aylmer flight commanders. This veteran came in one windless afternoon and groundlooped his Harvard right in front of his own hangar, doing considerable damage. He climbed out, lined up his entire flight and gave himself the most profane chewing they had ever heard. Then he fined himself twice the usual Rumble Fund assessment for landing damage. This was the spirit at Aylmer, tough but fair.

The Harvard was the perfect advanced trainer for fighter pilots. It was constructed, and it handled, like the top fighters of the day. Fly this ship properly, they'd tell us, and you can fly any single-engine type we've got, and this was a fair statement. The Harvard was easy to fly, but fast enough to sharpen your reflexes and demanding enough to keep you awake. And every hop ended with a grand chance to smash wingtips, bend the prop or even wipe off the gear completely.

On solo hops we were assigned certain practices to perform. It might be a cross-country one day and routine air work the next. There was ample time left over during each period for experimentation and it was expected that we would wring the ships out and make ourselves more or less at home in any aerial situation. At the noon mess Baldwin or Vogel might remark out the side of his mouth, "You're flying solo at 1400, aren't you?"

"What do you have in mind?"

"Meet you over Tillsonburg at 8,000."

"I'll be there at 1430."

Dogfighting was discouraged but not exactly forbidden. It could bring you a session with the flight commander or even the Old Man but it rarely meant washout, as was often the case with low flying. The main thing was not to get caught. There was not much secrecy about what was going on for the air near Aylmer on a sunny afternoon was filled with Harvards howling and

6147th Tactical Control Group LT-6 taxiing in at K-6 airfield, Korea, 1952. (Photo: G. M. Cameron)

6147th pilot prepares for a mission. Note the "armament" ...twelve 2.25 in. smoke rockets and a .45 caliber automatic pistol. (Photo: G. M. Cameron)

Lt. G. M. "Casey" Cameron (left) is congratulated on the completion of his 100th combat mission by Captain Anderson, the Group Operations Officer. (Photo: G. M. Cameron)

Italian Air Force T-6 in the inverted position for the benefit of a movie cameraman in the back seat of S2.62. (Photo: Italian Air Force; the Nagtegaal Collection)

twisting through awkward maneuvers as they tried to shoot each other down. There was no sport like it. I recall one such experience vividly for reasons which will become clear.

I got off the ground a few minutes early, scrambled rapidly to a thousand feet above the agreed level of engagement — such a deviation was not considered dishonorable — and lurked behind a big cumulus, waiting for my prey to appear at the point of rendezvous. Right on time and right on altitude he appeared, flying from the direction of the base. Craftily working my way around the cloud I got behind him with the sun at my back. Then, mentally flicking on the gun switch, I rolled on my back, Hell's Angels style, and dived for his tail.

I was McCudden, he was Von Richthofen. I pulled out a quarter of a mile behind him and the accumulated speed reduced the distance between us rapidly. I gave him a quick squirt, conserving my ammunition for another kill, and rolled away to his left — but not before I got a horrifying glimpse of *two* heads in the canopy. I had jumped a "D" Flight instructor and student. I rolled into a vertical dive for the nearest cloud bank. The Harvard burst from the clammy moisture and I eased it from the above-red line speed showing on the ASI. He couldn't have taken my number. It was all over too fast. Shaken, I decided to spend the rest of my time doing what Sergeant Campbell had sent me up to do.

But something made me look over my shoulder. There, not fifty feet behind, was a big fat 600 horsepower Pratt and Whitney engine. There were two helmeted heads in the cockpit. I put everything in the corner and away we went. For five minutes I flung myself about the air in every stunt I thought I knew but I didn't have a prayer. The big black engine on the slender yellow wing followed me like a shadow. At last I dropped the gear and permitted the "D" ship to come alongside. Two unsmiling faces regarded me coldly and then the Harvard banked away. I waited all evening for a summons to the C. O.'s office. None came. The next day Sergeant Campbell remarked, in passing, "Did you ever stop to think that a Harvard with one man in it should be able to *outclimb a* Harvard with two men in it?"

Nineteen is an impressionable age. Put a nineteen year old boy who has never wanted to do anything but fly in a big, hefty, fully-aerobatic 600 horsepower fighter-

Square-cut, all-yellow RCAF Harvards became a familiar sight over much of Canada as the British Commonwealth Air Training Plan gathered momentum. (Photo: North American Aviation)

Dutch T-6A pilot starts a roll.
(Photo: Royal Netherlands Air Force; the Nagtegaal Collection)

type airplane and he soaks up this new world like a sponge. The heady aroma of gasoline and dope, the spine-tingling sound of aircraft engines coming to life at sunrise, the utterly indescribable sensation at the top of a loop, the talk of those who speak your language, the snug feel of parachute straps, the entire overwhelming atmosphere at a busy flying field, the knowledge that you must no longer regard all of this through a fence. Professional airmen can always tell you more about the first two ships they flew than about many they have flown in the last five years.

What vivid recollections remain of those flying hours! The cockpit drill . . . three shots of prime, clear the prop, foot on the starter pedal between the rudders. Heel down to wind up the inertia starter, toe down to engage the clutch, switch on and maintain fuel pressure with the wobble pump. The sudden trembling of the big round cowl, the shimmering silver prop, the throttle adjustment to stabilize rpm at 800.

The Harvard taxied beautifully but it was necessary to zigzag in order to see around the engine. Weaver of "A" Flight was almost killed when a careless student, not zigzagging properly, sliced off his rudder and ran a wing right up behind his head before he got it stopped. A close one, that.

I remember it all . . . the final cockpit drill, brakes set, runup with the stick back to keep the tail down. Line up on the runway and roll forward to let the tailwheel lock and ease forward on the ball-handled throttle until the manifold pressure read 36 inches. The tail coming up, keep her straight with rudder, the controls stiffen quickly, ease back, off the runway, gear up, climbing nicely, work throttle and pitch controls to climbing power. Climbing out fast now with the trees dropping away beneath. Relax a bit. Turn left to leave traffic. Watch for other ships. This is living.

Level out at 9,000. Set up cruise power. Lean the mixture and recheck the fuel. Full tanks. Now what? This Harvard is not a straight and level airplane. It doesn't put you in the mood for 30 degree turns or letdowns with the vertical speed nailed on 500 feet a minute. All that rot is for the Anson crowd over at Brantford. This is a fun airplane. OK, let's go . . .

Nose over abruptly and lift yourself up against the straps. Watch the airspeed walk around to 200. Ease back, not too hard. You hear a loud rush of air past the windscreen and are jammed hard onto the chute. The controls are rigid and require muscle. The big nose rises obediently and the horizon drops from sight and now there's nothing but blue sky everywhere. Easy, don't stall it. The speed drops rapidly, the roar of air disappears and all is quiet except for the vibrating, laboring engine and the thrashing prop. Upside down and you're weightless, neither sitting in your chute nor hanging from the straps. A delicious, exhiliarating instant and then the nose falls through slowly and the speed gathers. The horizon reappears from overhead and there is again a tremendous roar of air and nothing but green fields before the nose. Easy, easy . . . don't pull it too tight. Leveling out at the bottom. A sudden severe bump as you slice through your own propwash. You settle back and allow the speed to dwindle.

Let's try it again, with variations. Nose over and speed climbing to 220 this time. A great sound of rushing air and the stick feeling like it's set in concrete. Ease back and stick yourself hard on the chute; couldn't raise your feet now if you tried. The horizon drops away and there's nothing but clear blue sky everywhere. Look back and watch for the horizon coming up from behind the tail . . . there it is. Now, stick all the way over, some rudder to hold the nose up — and roll out on top. Immelmann did it first, they say.

Now, let's do a roll. No wait! Here comes American Airlines. That fat old DC-3 looks tempting, plodding along down there at 165. Should we? It's absolutely against the regulations and the Old Man is out stooging about somewhere in the area. While we hesitate to ponder the odds, two Harvards, their bright yellow wings flashing in the sunshine, fall from above in loose formation, fire imaginery bursts from six machine guns and hurtle earthward into the undercast without breaking their dive. They beat us to it.

RCAF Harvard IIA. (Photo: Canadian Department of National Defense)

Green Airway Number Two connected Detroit with Buffalo in those days and its centerline lay right across Aylmer. Several times a day American DC-3s made this run and we figured that the big airliners were as much invaders of our private bit of air as the clumsy Ansons, piloted by former St. Kitts classmates, that sometimes wandered over to see what we were up to. It was strictly forbidden to jump an Anson, much less American Airlines. But to permit this brash trespassing to proceed unchallenged was unthinkable, particularly when a well-placed cloud bank promised refuge after the attack. After all, we were supposed to be training for combat, weren't we?

The miracle of it is that American's brave crews flew that run throughout the war without colliding with a headstrong student even though the route fell within the training areas of several RCAF stations. Then, one rainy night while every Harvard pilot in Southern Ontario was whooping it up in his wet canteen, an American DC-3 took a goose right through the windshield and went down a few miles east of Aylmer. That goose had twenty-four numbers on it.

The RCAF was keen on spin recovery. The word from England was that combat pilots were spinning out of the perpetual winter overcast and dying simply because there was not enough room below the clouds for recovery. We spun Fleets from the first day and when we had mastered this they put us under the hood in the back seat and made us pull out with needle, ball and airspeed. On each solo hop we were supposed to do at least one spin and mark it on the chart in ops when we landed. At Aylmer it was the same — dual spins contact and under the hood, and a spin on every solo hop with a place to put a check mark on a chart.

The time's running out so we'll spin off this altitude south of the field and join the circuit. Make a 360 to clear ourselves. Throttle back all the way, engine just ticking over. It's very quiet except for air noise around the canopy.

Hold the altitude as speed falls off. The nose rises. The ASI reads 85 . . . 80 . . . 75. It's deathly quiet. A tremble followed immediately by a violent shudder which makes the instrument panel jump crazily on its rubber mounts. The left wing drops and the nose falls like a brick and swings sharply to the left. Stick back all the way; hold full rudder. The landscape's gone insane with houses, roads and lakes swimming in a nauseating circle. The nose rises a little but the rapid, jerking spin continues. The altimeter unwinds unevenly, 300 feet at a time. Airspeed reading about 70 when you can find it. Dust all over the place and a blue pencil floating by your nose. Four turns, five, six. Altitude slipping through 6,000 feet. Time to recover. Does the book say start recovery at five or six? Never mind, the ground's rushing up too fast anyway and this thing is wrapped up tight. Here goes . . .

Stick full forward and full opposite rudder. You talk out loud to restore sanity to the situation. Shove for-

AT-6s and BT-14s on the line at North American Aviation. (Photo: North American Aviation)

ward and brace that leg. The wild, jerking rotation continues unabated for another full turn then, with a final shuddering wrench, the nose aims itself at a red barn and the wings snap back to level. Neutralize immediately or she'll spin the other way. Let the speed build and bring the power in. Fly level and let everything stabilize.

Drop down to 1700 feet and squeeze into the string of yellow ships lining up on downwind leg. H-T-M-P-C-G-T. Speed 125. Gear down and check the indicators. Left base with speed at 100. Turn onto final. Speed 90. You notice a Harvard on another runway standing on its nose. Probably tried to stop a groundloop. Will the ship ahead clear in time? Yes, there's the green light. Cut the throttle and let it settle. Wheels on the runway, tail dropping. Watch it, watch it! Easy on that rudder! Tailwheel digging in; use the brakes; turn off the strip and taxi in, zigzagging carefully. Ease up to the line at "C" Flight's hangar, kick hard rudder and give her a burst. Line up with the others. Run the prop into coarse pitch and shut down. Walk into the hangar weary in body but feeling like a million bucks.

"Morgan, you're night flying at 2000 hours. Report here at 1930."

"Solo, Sarge?"

"No, I'm going with you. We'll do some spin recoveries."

This was the life for a nineteen year old.

In later years I often compared notes with Army and Navy trained pilots to see how our training stacked up against theirs. Army pilots trained prior to 1942 recall that as underclassmen they sat on the edges of their mess chairs, in the manner of West Point plebes, were frequently braced by their seniors and ran from class to class with arms outstretched like birds, "banking" on the turns. This sophmoric nonsense was eliminated after Pearl Harbor. It was never a part of the picture in the RCAF in 1941, though it may well have been in prewar days. In 1941 Canada was a partner with Britain in war and the main idea was to train as many aircrew members as possible in the shortest possible time consistent with quality. Our training was hurried but it covered the essentials thoroughly. Looking back, I am surprised that such a practical and sensible approach to flight instruction could have been devised by any military service. Necessity is the mother of invention and the chips were down for the British Empire.

The author in a "C" Flight Harvard of No. 14 Service Flying Training School, Aylmer, Ontario.

Our groundschool subjects were for the most part pertinent, though we did waste valuable hours learning to swing a compass and send Morse code on an Aldis lamp. Every military-trained pilot I know has spent hours at code practice, learning something no more than five percent of them ever used. The Morse-code-for-pilots craze died a hard death — that is, if it ever did die. Perhaps they still put cadets into those stalls and make them learn to take ten words a minute.

Flight training was strictly no-nonsense. We were taught to take off and land without damaging His Maj-

Factory-fresh T-6D. This was the most widely used model in the United States. A total of 4388 were produced. They performed a wide variety of tasks including pilot instruction, fixed and flexible gunnery training, and target towing. (Photo: North American Aviation)

esty's property, aeroplanes, hangars or otherwise, to navigate by day or night, to fly on instruments and handle our ships in any average situation. That's about it. Army pilots speak of "precision spins," "overhead 360s," "pylon eights" and "spot landings." I've never been quite sure what they are talking about. The RCAF theory was that a student fighter pilot should *not* be taught precision aerobatics. Our instructors, if pressed, would show us a Cuban Eight or a snap roll or slow roll but they pointed out that precision flight has no place in combat. Fly a precise path and the German knew exactly where you were going — and he would shoot you down. The erratic, uncordinated, slipping, skidding plane presents the most difficult target. At least, this was the way the Canadians saw it and they had formed this opinion during the Battle of Britain.

The RCAF curriculum included perhaps three hours of aerobatic dual, an hour of formation and no radio work at all. Our ships were not equipped with radio gear of any description. Airport traffic was controlled by lights operated by an instructor at the end of the runway. American Army and Navy students, even during accelerated wartime training, received considerable aerobatic instruction, formation experience and radio work. The American cadet was a better trained pilot when he got his wings than we were, but only because the BCATP intended that its graduates receive further training after graduation. RCAF graduates were sent to England for further instruction at Operational Training Units, these courses sometimes adding 100 to 150 additional hours to the student's logbook. In the case of Harvard graduates, this meant four to twelve weeks on Hurricanes or Spits during which period combat tactics, formation and radio procedures were taught. Then came assignment to an operational unit where, insofar as the current situation allowed, new men were sent on routine patrols or other milk run assignments until they were skilled in fighter methods. Boiled down, the RCAF student got his wings at an earlier stage of his overall training than his American counterpart. The final product in either case was reasonably competent and able to carry his own weight in a front line outfit.

Speaking of our American counterparts reminds me that Selfridge Field, that hallowed center of pursuit aviation, was but a few flying minutes from Aylmer and, whereas Air Corps pilots were forbidden to wander across the international line, they were fighter men just as we were striving to be. So it was that on a certain August afternoon I found a dazzling new P-38 sitting on one wing, and a wicked-looking P-40 on the other. We flew along this way for several minutes looking each other over before the Air Corps types turned away for their base. I imagined that they might be a bit envious of me at that moment, even though my yellow Harvard was no match for their mounts. But, as it turned out, they were not far behind us in our eastward journey to the war.

A couple of Harvards from another station ventured across the lake about sundown one evening and worked over the municipal airport at Erie, Pennsylvania. This resulted in a number of international phone calls, stern lectures by all C. O.'s and words of warning from every instructor.

A week later another Harvard student dropped in at Detroit's busy airline terminal, enjoyed a leisurely cup of coffee and was gone before anyone realized who he was. More phone calls from Washington to Ottawa, more stern lectures, more warnings. This sort of thing was never-ending. More than one honeymooning couple standing on International Bridge at Niagara Falls was unnerved by the sudden sight of a Fleet or Harvard or even a rattling old Anson roaring beneath their feet and disappearing into the dusk before any numbers could be copied down.

When these things happened we would be mustered for parade in full dress. After a great deal of marching about, dressing up the ranks and standing at attention in the sun, the Old Man would appear.

"Does anyone here have any knowledge whatsoever of two Harvard aircraft flying low over the city of Buffalo yesterday afternoon at (looking at his telegram) approximately 1630 hours?"

Silence.

North American BT-14, one of the predecessors of the AT-6 series. (Photo: North American Aviation)

AT-6A. (Photo: North American Aviation)

AT-6C. (Photo: North American Aviation)

AT-6D. (Photo: North American Aviation)

XAT-6E...this was a modified AT-6D with a Ranger V-770-9 575 h. p. high-altitude engine.
(Photo: North American Aviation)

AT-6F. (Photo: North American Aviation)

T-6G. (Photo: North American Aviation)

In 1951 the Harvard Mk. IV was introduced into RCAF service. This was basically a Mk. II with advanced instrumentation and communication equipment, greater fuel capacity, and better visibility for the crew. It was similar to the USAF's remanufactured T-6G. (Photo: Canadian Department of National Defense)

"Thirty-two of our machines were airborne at that time. No information on this from any of you people?"

Silence, except for someone in the back row of "C" flight quietly clearing his throat.

"Very well, then. Sergeant Major, dismiss the parade."

And, later in the mess.

"I say, Rodney, did you hear the Squadron Leader and that sticky business about aeroplanes flying over Buffalo, or wherever that American place is?"

"He took a dim view of that, didn't he? It couldn't have been any of our chaps, of course."

Canadian voice. "Where were you two Limeys all afternoon anyway?"

"We did our cross-country to Windsor, old boy. Christopher was on my wing all the way, weren't you, Chris?"

"Indeed I was. You don't think we had anything to do with this Buffalo thing do you? Sounds more like something a couple of irresponsible Yanks would do. How about it, Wynne?"

"I'm from Georgia, Don't call me 'Yank.' I was on a navigation hop myself."

"Where to?"

"Never mind. It was probably some Canadians anyway. They can't find their way to the bathroom. Probably thought they were over Toronto."

"Wait a minute. Doesn't Wee Willie Wendt know some girl in Buffalo?"

"Hold it, men, hold it! I know what you're thinking. Do you think I could stand there in front of my Commanding Officer and hold my tongue if I knew anything about this awful violation of the rules?"

"I believe he could, Rodney, don't you?"

"Quite possibly. Where is this Minnesota place he comes from?"

"One of the colonies, somewhere in the Pacific. Captain Cook and all that, you know."

Of course, we all knew who had buzzed Buffalo.

In spite of our accelerated training schedule there was time for "outside activities" away from the base. As long as we passed the weekly groundschool exams and weather did not delay flying, the weekends were free from duty. Toronto, Detroit and Buffalo were the usual targets. To stand on the highway in an RCAF uniform was to get a lift from the first car along which helped when you earned seventy dollars a month. The Canadian people could not have been more friendly or generous to us. As often as not you'd get invited home for din-

Harvard IIA taxiing out at Uplands. Traffic was usually heavy at the training stations. In this photo three Harvards can be seen on final approach. (Photo: Canadian Department of National Defense)

Harvard IV. After more than 25 years of service, RCAF Harvards were retired from the training role in 1965. (Photo: Canadian Car and Foundry Company)

ner, or the weekend. I have the most pleasant recollections of those footloose weekends and of the genuine warmth and friendliness of the local people I met. We Americans are fortunate to have them as neighbors.

The weeks flew by. We sweated at navigation and aero engines. We roared across the land in our Harvards, wheeling around the billowing cumulus in exhilirating chases, now relaxed behind the howling six hundred horses and even dreaming now and then of something that would climb more steeply and cruise faster. If there is a finer sport than play among the clouds in a stout and agile plane I have yet to hear of it. It was completely illegal and downright dangerous when two were involved, but what tremendous fun! If you were nineteen then and one of the lucky few at Aylmer you didn't worry much about what was in the book as long as there was a chance to get by with it and — as I have remarked — our mentors knew when to look the other way. The hazard involved was a spice we required at that stage of the game.

"You'll look back someday and know that these were the best days of all your flying," Mr. Bennett had said. In a way he was right. But only in one way for any pilot, thumbing through the brittle pages of old logbooks will catch himself thinking, again and again, *these* were the best days, though I did not know it then. The sum total of impressions, the hazy swirl of individual recollections, punctuated here and again by vivid memories of inexpressible pleasure, fear beyond description or sudden tragedy — this is the memory that pleases him and haunts him. The Harvard is at once the wondrous vehicle that unlocked a new world, and a hideous, mud-spattered heap of yellow aluminum that snuffed out the life of a luckless friend. This is the way we remember it.

The dreaded "washing machine ride" continued to take its toll, though never at the rate we had known in Elementary. Three from "C" Flight got the axe and were posted to navigator's school. Those of us remaining received our wings on November 21 and were given ten days of leave before going overseas.

That might have been the end of the Harvard story for me but the fortunes of war and the unfathomable ways of peace lead us into unexpected situations. There was more of the scene to be played.

CANADIAN—TRAINED AIRCREW GRADUATES OF THE BRITISH COMMONWEALTH AIR TRAINING PLAN

Trade	RCAF	RAF	RAAF	RNZAF	Total
Pilot	25,747	17,796	4,045	2,200	49,808
Navigator	12,855	13.882	1,643	1,583	29,963
Air Bomber	6,659	7,581	799	634	15,673
Wireless Operator/ Air Gunner	12,744	755	2,875	2,122	18,496
Naval Air Gunner		704			704
Air Gunner	12,917	1,392	244	443	14,996
Flight Engineer	1,913				1,913
Totals	72,835	42,110	9,606	7,002	131,553

RCAF - Royal Canadian Air Force
RAF - Royal Air Force
RAAF - Royal Australian Air Force
RNZAF - Royal New Zealand Air Force

Source — Wing Commander R. V. Manning, Air Historian, Department of National Defense, Ottawa

Flying Harvard IVs, the "Goldilocks" aerobatic team entertained at air shows throughout Canada during 1962 - 1964. One of the highlights of the team's performance was the "crazy formation", demonstrated below. (Photos: Canadian Department of National Defense)

Friend and Foe... World War II

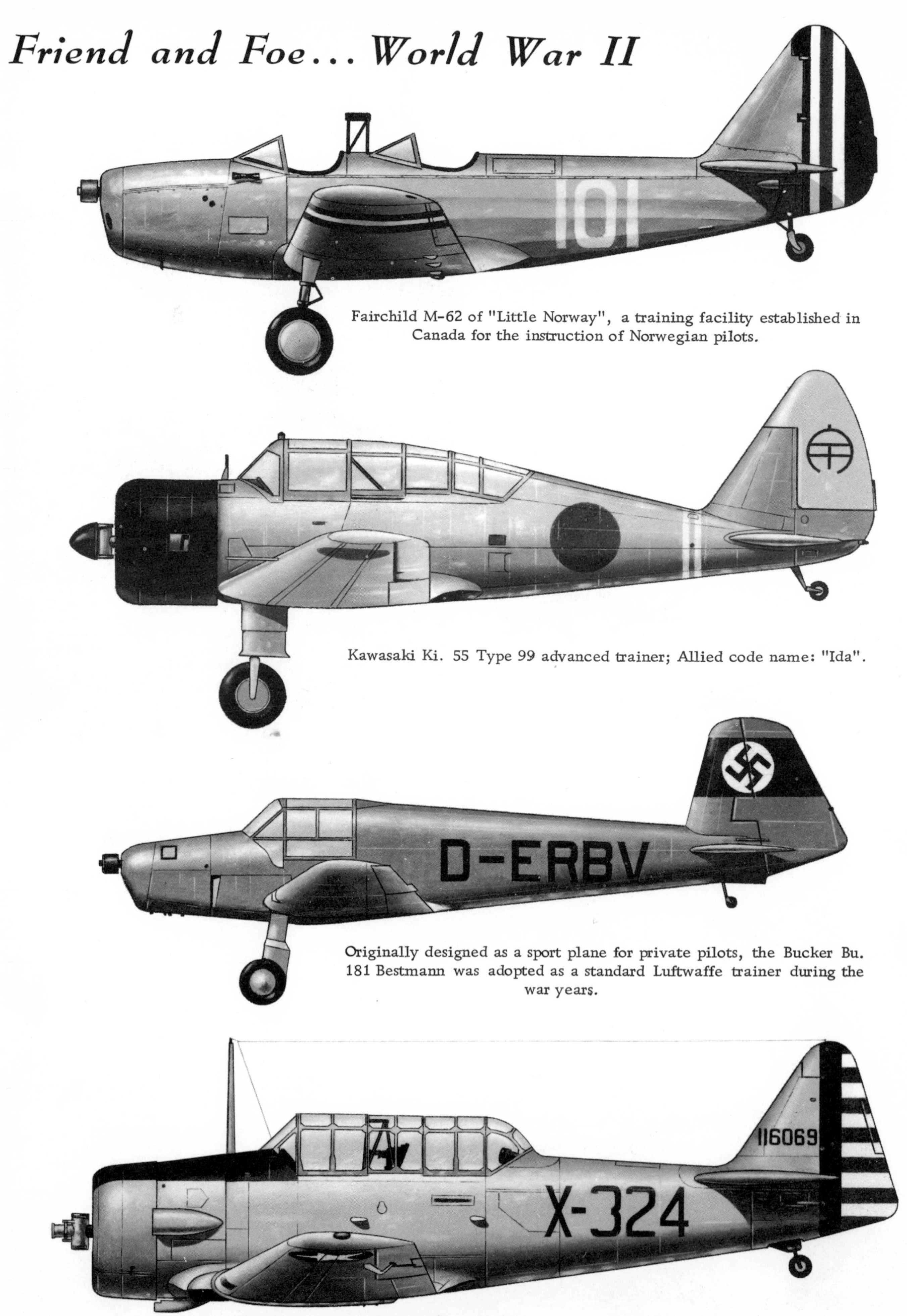

Fairchild M-62 of "Little Norway", a training facility established in Canada for the instruction of Norwegian pilots.

Kawasaki Ki. 55 Type 99 advanced trainer; Allied code name: "Ida".

Originally designed as a sport plane for private pilots, the Bucker Bu. 181 Bestmann was adopted as a standard Luftwaffe trainer during the war years.

This AT-6A performed dual flight instruction duty at Luke Field, Arizona.

U.S. Development and Service Roles

This AT-6A gunnery trainer served at Harlingen Field, Texas during World War II.

A veteran of the gunnery school at Hondo, Texas, this T-6D was mustered out of service in 1957. It is now owned by Captain Robert O'Hara who flies it in the No. 2 position in "A" Flight of the Civil Air Patrol's 35th Air Rescue Squadron, based at San Fernando, California.

Civilian T-6F. This very beautifully decorated ship was recorded at Van Nuys Airport, Van Nuys, California.

T-6G of the Massachusetts Air National Guard. Remanufacturing of this "D" model to the "G" configuration was done at North American's Fresno, California plant. This ship was among the last 60 T-6s of a total of 2068 to undergo the remanufacturing process.

Whether it was called the AT-6...

...the Harvard...

...or the SNJ, the only external difference was usually found in the markings. (Photos: North American Aviation)

"Will It Go To 22,000?"

During the war the Harvard — or AT-6, as we began calling it after we had transferred to the Army — was a familiar sight on Allied airfields all over the world. There was almost always one or two parked near operations. They were used by the administrative crowd for cross-countries and instrument practice and by gravel agitators logging the four monthly hours required for flight pay. Any base pilot chummy enough with this clique could borrow one for an hour's fun.

Flying the AT-6 was no different from flying the Harvard but the language changed. Airscrew and undercart became prop and landing gear; circuits-and-bumps became touch-and-goes; you didn't prang the kite anymore, you clobbered the ship; of course, if you were so unfortunate as to write yourself off, you had bought the farm in either air force. We now ran checklists instead of doing takeoff drills and looked through the windshield instead of the windscreen; gas was measured in U. S. gallons while petrol had been listed in Imperial. But standing there on the ramp/tarmac or any military field/aerodome, the AT-6/Harvard was the same airplane/aeroplane it had always been — and that's the straight poop from group/pukka gen, fellows/chaps. And it groundlooped/groundlooped just as easily.

After the war ended the reserve units got them and you waited around half the day to fly one, exchanging shop talk with P-38 and P-51 pilots. It was better than nothing. Those were the dismal days when the airlines were accepting one pilot from each fifty applicants. Men who had led bomber squadrons into Italy were instructing GI schools, flying 75 horsepower puddle jumpers, and happy to have the job. It was not a good time to be a pilot.

Purely by chance I learned of a steady job that promised a little flying. The work was that of flying for a company engaged in aerial mapping. The owner had been engaged in this pursuit in the 1930s and had built an excellent reputation. He had operated Cessna C-165 Airmasters, this type being ideally suited to the unusual demands of the work. After Pearl Harbor he had shut down, sold his fleet of mappers and taken a high rank in the Army. He was just reopening shop when luck brought us together.

"What's the highest you've ever flown an AT-6?" he asked.

I said about 15,000 feet.

"Will it go to 22,000 with two men aboard?"

I said it might, though I doubted it.

"I've got one at the field. Let's go find out."

The ship he had bought surplus was not technically an AT-6, as it turned out, but a BC-1A. To walk around it and examine it, inside and out, you would never guess it was anything but a plain vanilla AT-6 like all the other hundreds you had seen. But it had another half foot of wingspan, slightly more fuel capacity and a higher allowable gross weight (by 150 pounds, as I recall) than the regular model. The boss had had small medical oxygen bottles installed with nasal masks. We climbed in and took off and I reminded myself that I hadn't flown one of these things in several months.

The ship lifted us smartly to 5,000 feet, more slowly to 10,000 and was laboring by the time we showed 15,000. But it still indicated a 300 feet per minute climb and had considerable life left. Forty-five minutes after takeoff we struggled through 20,000, still climbing but at a

September 26, 1946. The author flying BC-1A, NX-61790, over the Continental Divide at 22,700 feet.

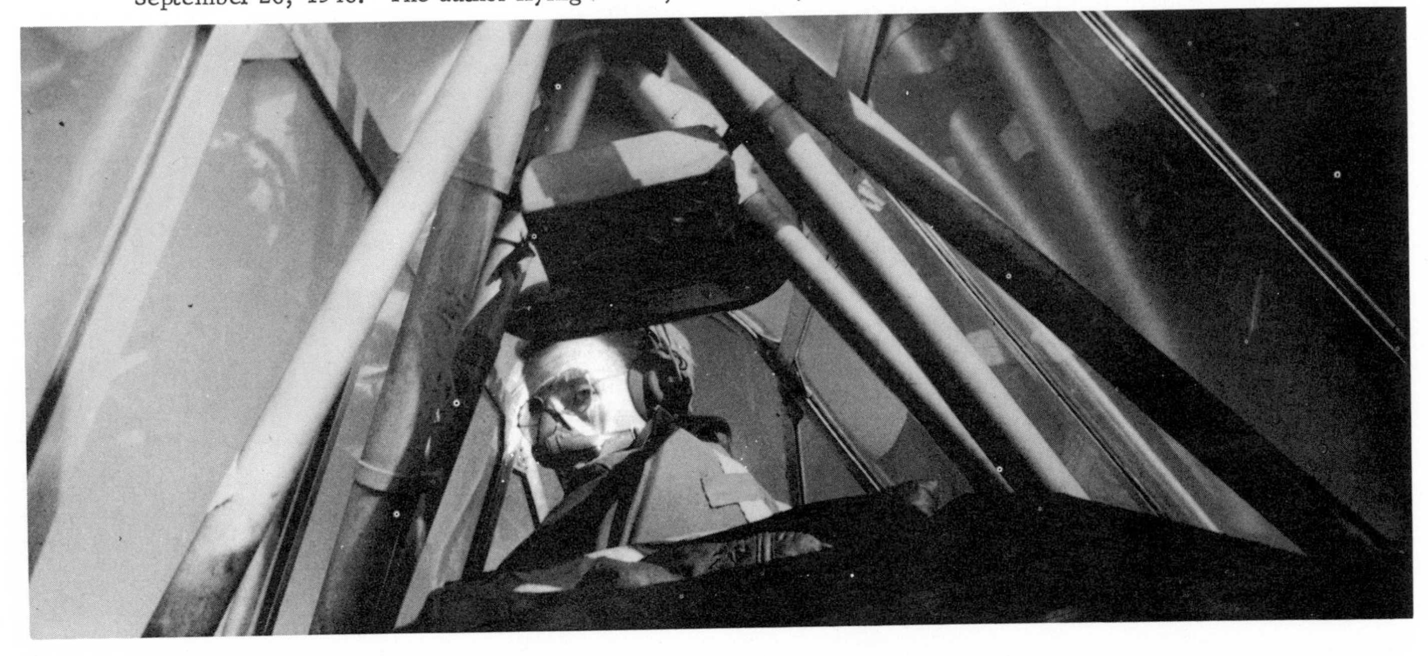

The T-6G was a rebuilt version of older T-6C and D models, completely remanufactured to meet requirements of the early nineteen-fifties. The only apparent external differences from older models included a square-tipped propellor to reduce noise level, single-pane cockpit windows for improved visibility, metal-covered ailerons elevators, and rudder, new and relocated antenna and pitot-masts, and F-51 type steerable tailwheel. All armament was removed. Internally, instrumentation was standardized and interchangeable in both cockpits, fuel capacity was increased, and advanced communication equipment was installed. (Photo: North American Aviation)

painfully slow rate. Manifold pressure had dropped to 17 inches and we advanced rpm, which helped a bit. At 21,000 we were barely hanging in the sky, but it was still possible with careful nursing to keep the vertical speed needle on the top side of the "0." The last thousand feet took nine minutes.

"Trying leveling off and getting the best rpm setting," he said through the intercom.

I fiddled with prop and mixture, attempting to get the last ounce of thrust from the engine. The ship staggered along, tail down, nibbling at the stall but hung tenaciously to the 22,000 feet it had attained.

"Make a 180 degree turn."

We dropped the wing five degrees and slopped through it, losing 300 feet, the stick quivering all the while as we threatened to stall.

"Try another." We cut the altitude loss to 100 feet.

I was beginning to get the feel of it now, flying the ship on half power within a mile or two of its stalling speed. Further experimentation with the rpm made it fly even better.

"It'll do," he announced. "Take me down."

The ship was pulled into the hangar and the mechanics went to work, stripping out the back seat, floor boards, baggage bin — everything that did not affect airworthiness. We went over the ship from prop to tail light, removing all radio masts, shortening drain pipes and vents, taping holes. All paint except the anti-glare panel and NC numbers was scraped off. A large hole, about twenty inches square, was cut in the belly of the back cockpit and a plexiglass window installed. A camera mount was attached and racks for rolls of film. New

After the war, the T-6 served in many varied roles and modifications; a few of these are illustrated below.

U. S. Navy SNJ-4 (Photo: North American Aviation)

Civilian racing conversion of the XAT-6E. (Photo: North American Aviation)

T-6G of the New Hampshire Air National Guard. (Photo: the Nagtegaal Collection)

Single-seat racing conversion of the basic AT-6 design. (Photo: the Nagtegaal Collection)

T-6 used by the Dutch Skylight Company in Holland for skywriting. (Photo: the Nagtegaal Collection)

T-6D of the 35th Air Rescue Squadron, Civil Air Patrol. (Official Oxnard AFB Photo)

and heavier oxygen bottles were clamped to the cross braces between the seats. A small floor and seat was fitted for the photographer.

We filled the tanks and tried it again, this time with a full working load aboard. Sixty-five minutes after breaking ground we were level at 22,000 feet and doing 180s with no loss in altitude. We watched one of Eastern's flashy new Connies cross beneath us on the hotshot run to Atlanta and wondered if its crew saw us.

"It'll do nicely," the boss repeated and we dropped down to land.

Aerial mapping is the world's safest flying job. To obtain satisfactory vertical photographs of the earth's surface you must have almost perfect flight conditions. The slightest amount of smoke or haze, any cloud whatsoever or even a suggestion of turbulence makes the day unsuitable for this work. All photography must be completed at least three hours after sunrise and not later than three hours before sunset. These are the minimum weather conditions for the aerial mapping pilot. The result is that he works no more than four days a month even in such good weather areas as Kansas and Texas. In Washington and Oregon and other coastal regions he is lucky to get a half day of suitable weather a month, on the average. It is not uncommon for a photographic job requiring five days of flying to stretch out for the length of a summer. The mapping pilot never flies at night or in any form of weather. One tiny cumulus puff on the horizon at sunrise cancels the day's work.

Aerial mapping calls for perhaps the most precise navigation known in aviation. A mapping pilot carries a large scale county map of the area he wishes to shoot. On it are drawn in red pencil the "lines" he has to fly to obtain suitable photographs. The tolerance for error differs from job to job but it is not unusual for the maximum allowable deviation from a line to be eight hundred feet. Try this from 22,000 feet!

Lines are normally flown on North and South headings. This permits the prevailing west winds to force the ship into a crabbing track which, in turn, gets the nose out of the way and provides a better view of the earth. The stronger the wind the better, as long as it's steady.

It is the mapping pilot's job to put his photographer right over each line, stay over it for its entire length and to fly smoothly and without variations in heading or altitude. It's an art. The photographer, crouched over his big camera, levels it with bubble sights, shoots, winds in the next frame and — exactly at the right time interval — shoots again. This is also an art. The interval is determined with a drift meter and is such that the forward overlap of pictures is about fifty percent. Sidelap runs thirty on most jobs. Overlap is the photographer's concern, sidelap the pilot's.

An oblique photograph exposed at 23,000 feet over the Continental Divide. The Forest Lakes in the foreground, Denver in the distance. September, 1946.

This is a task requiring much patience, a keen eye for ground detail and the knack for imagining that the red line on your map is actually down there, crossing that bridge, running beside that railroad and up the side of that hill. An expert mapper (there are pilots who are naturals at this strange work) can fly his lines with amazing accuracy, turn off them exactly at each end and resume level flight seconds later going the opposite way, exactly above the next line.

A sharp photographer can operate his clumsy camera automatically, reload it while the ship swings around at the end of the job and help with the tricky navigation.

"You are drifting east. Give me two degrees right." Or, "There's a couple of clouds forming in the west. What say we cut over four lines and pick up the one running through those two small lakes, then work back this way and get the others before it folds?" The weather "folds up" for a mapping crew when a cloud the size of a barn is seen below or when industrial smoke cuts visibility to eight miles or less.

The photographs obtained in this manner are used in a hundred ways. Cities use them for traffic studies, highway planning and in the master plans for expansion. These jobs are small, it being quite easy to map a place like Nashville or Cincinnati in a couple of hours, if everything goes right, but we did them when we were near a city needing a fresh set of pictures. Our bread and butter was the large contract for a federal agency which wanted ten to forty counties mapped. Such a project will keep a crew or two busy all summer.

After a few small practice jobs close to base my photographer and I set off on our first major project, the mapping of a sizeable area of Colorado mountains including the Continental Divide. This work had been contracted by the U. S. Forest Service which used the photos to measure water in remote lakes, seek out and identify tree diseases, count deer and bring their maps of mountain roads and trails up to date. We inspected the ship and our photographic gear carefully and began the long wait.

We met at Stapleton Field each clear morning just after sunrise, ran up the engine and topped the tanks. Two hours after sunrise we were off the ground and climbing to the west, nursing the ship to get the most rapid rate of ascent. On the first nine flights the same thing happened. Almost exactly at the legal starting time we'd see tiny cumulus clouds popping into existence in the mountain valleys. Incidentally, there's no opportunity to fudge at the game. The experts with their special viewing equipment can tell exactly when a picture was exposed and almost to the foot the altitude from which it was shot. It was all right to be above the stipulated 22,000 feet, but anything taken more than 100 feet below was rejected.

On the tenth try we managed to run off two lines before the cumulus appeared. We airmailed the film

Trainers Then and Now

(All drawn to the same scale)

The Maurice Farman M. F. 11 "Shorthorn" was the most widely used trainer of the British Royal Flying Corps in the early years of World War I. It had a loaded weight of 2,046 lb. and turned in a blistering top speed of 66 m. p. h. at sea level.

The Consolidated PT-3A was the standard U. S. Army trainer of the nineteen-thirties. Loaded weight was 2,432 lb. Top speed had climbed to 102 m. p. h.

Harvard IIA of the Royal New Zealand Air Force. The wartime Harvard weighed more than twice as much as the PT-3. Maximum speed had also doubled to 205 m. p. h.

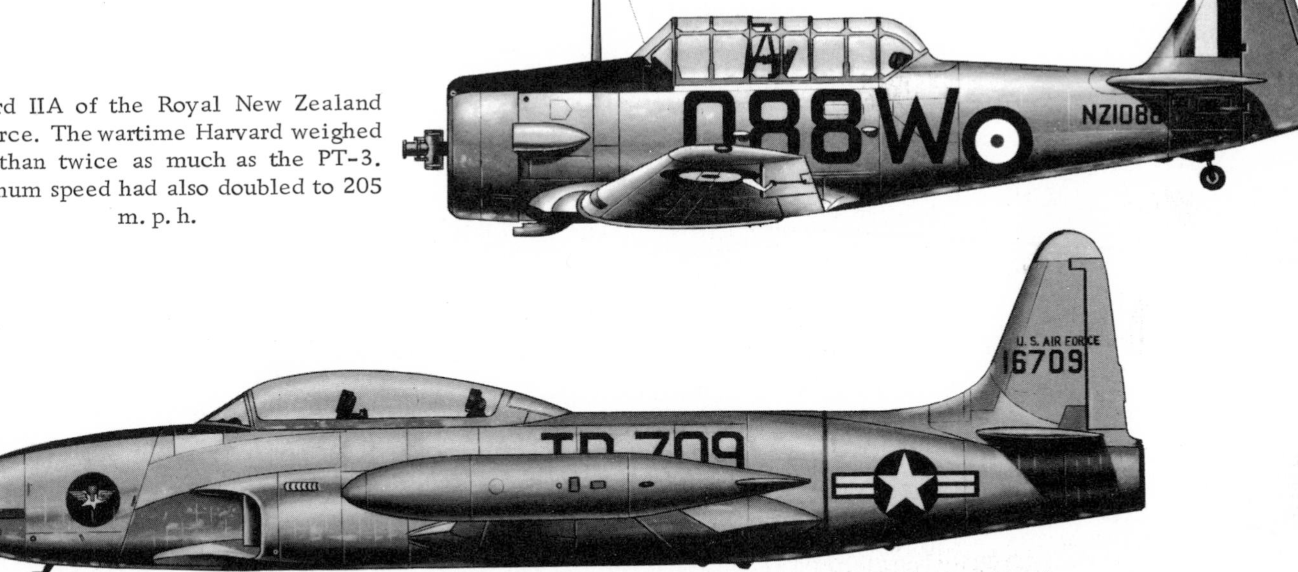

The Lockheed T-33 is one of the most famous and durable of all trainers. Originally developed in 1947, the "T-Bird", like the Harvard, is still flying in many air forces throughout the world. Maximum loaded weight is 14,482 lb. Top speed is 580 m. p. h. The aircraft illustrated is an Air Training Command ship which was based at Pine Castle AFB, Florida in 1952.

Northrop T-38 Talon. Today, USAF pilots are trained solely on jet aircraft. The primary student logs 132 hours in the Cessna T-37. He then goes on to advanced training in the T-38 which he flies a minimum of 120 hours before moving up to tactical aircraft. The T-38's maximum speed is 850 m. p. h.; loaded weight is 11,650 lb.

Idaho Springs, Colorado, from 23,000 feet. (Photo: U. S. Forest Service)

home for processing and in two days had a phone call from the boss. Not a single acceptable exposure; we had been too far off the lines. The photographer gave me a dirty look but said nothing.

Mapping crews in our outfit were paid a small base wage and made their real money in the form of bonuses paid on each mile successfully flown. The more times you reflew a line, the lower the bonus on it. When the sidelap was wrong the cameramen beefed; when the photographer had to reload in the middle of a line going particularly well, the pilot howled. Workwise, it required great patience. Paywise, it was chicken today and feathers tomorrow.

You waited three weeks to fly the twenty minutes that would wrap up a job. You scramble for height, cursing the old bucket for not climbing faster. You held the stick like you were repairing a watch and tried to stay exactly above a straight line that runs through twisting mountain valleys. You could only guess about the winds.

Aerial mapping as a science has advanced rapidly since that time. Supersonic fighters flash across the terrain at treetop level, a battery of automatic cameras recording every detail. With the pictures they produce you can tell if the enemy is keeping his shoes shined. Sometimes in the midwest at night you will see sudden brilliants flashes as reconnaissance crews practice night photography with magnesium flares. With infrared equipment they now map cities through cloud cover and come up with photos so sharp that locomotives can be counted in the stations.

The civilian operators in this field have moved on to faster equipment, the P-38 being used with some success despite its enormous thirst. But much of the work behind the roadmap you used on your last vacation was done by a lonely pair of half-frozen fellows who limped through the sky on the edge of a stall, so high you never saw or heard them. Theirs is an unusual way of life, an unknown corner of the total aviation picture, but their work affects us all.

My brief participation in this field was all the more interesting to me because it was accomplished in a plane I knew and admired. There may be better ways to earn a living then flying an AT-6; there are certainly worse ones.

This plane was never designed for anything like that. Its single-stage blower was never intended to supply fuel and air at 22,000 feet. Its blunt wing was not put together for those high levels. But plane and engine did the job and my admiration for each increased. On one flight when the fuel tanks were almost dry we actually got that old tub up to 24,000 feet indicated, a fact many of my Army and Navy friends have found hard to swallow. I would not have believed it myself.

The ship was as much a sheer delight as a workhorse as it had been when it was only the second airplane I'd ever flown. It would be just as much fun today. There are many of them still flying the world over. It's a fine sport plane for the private airman who has had his fill of these tricycle things they sell today. When that big Pratt and Whitney shakes itself into life you know you're strapped to a real piece of flying machinery.

My own interest in this great airplane — for it is just that, a great airplane — has been rekindled in the process of producing this short sketch. The other day, at a western airfield, I saw one near the terminal where we park and walked over to see it close. It was a beat-up wreck, with the many nicks and dents that time will leave on any plane. The big cowling was repaired in several places with strips of metal and a section of the rear fuselage had a crude patch on it. The old Air Force insignia still showed faintly on the dull silver sides, testimony to those distant days when this job sat in a long row of T-6s at some forgotten training field. There were signs of rust on the big Pratt's cylinders and a regrettable steady drip of oil forming a pool between the wheels. I climbed up on the wing and peered inside. There were gaping holes in the panel where instruments had been removed. The familiar controls and dials and cockpit fixtures had that faded, neglected look that is common to all tired old airplanes. A placard I did not comprehend had been riveted to the instrument panel. It read, "Intentional Spinning Prohibited." The heavy brown safety harness was frayed and greasy. It was, in its own private way in my mind, a rather sad sight.

I walked away, this attempted quick visit to the past having failed completely. When we came back two days later the battered T-6 was gone and a fancy new cabin job sat above the pool of oil it had left.

(Photo: the Nagtegaal Collection)

On the next two pages artist Richard Groh depicts a scene played countless times in Ontario during the early days of World War II. A solo student flying a Harvard based at No. 14 Service Flying Training School has spotted a Fleet student from No. 9 Elementary Flying Training School and is demonstrating what a real airplane will do. Both ships shown here were flown by the author during his own RCAF training days in 1941.

3064

4727

"the best scout trainer in the world."

The T-6 has been called "the most universally used airplane in history." It was the classroom from which most World War II Allied pilots graduated to the real thing: Thunderbolts, Spitfires, Corsairs, Mustangs. It was designed to provide the best possible training in all aspects of military flying including ground-strafing, dive-bombing, dogfighting, aerial photography, flexible gunnery, and it carried most of the equipment which pilots of the period had to operate. Lieutenant E. C. Dickinson, the most decorated Navy flier of the war, called the SNJ version "the best scout trainer in the world."

In addition to its outstanding training record, the T-6 has won battle honors the world over. In July, 1942, a T-6 scored two direct hits on a German submarine off the coast of Tampico . . . the sub was believed to have been sunk. In December of the same year an Australian version of the T-6, the Wirraway, shot down a Japanese Zero fighter over New Guinea. Unofficial sources credit an SNJ pilot with a similar feat in the Philippines. During the Korean War, LT-6s of the 6147th Tactical Control Group patrolled the communist side of the front, spotting and marking targets for faster fighter-bombers. One or two of the Group's ships were armed with a pair of .30 calibre machine guns and were used to "protect" the precious F-86s from night raids by Russian-designed PO-2 "Bed-Check Charlies." During the recent clash between Pathet Lao and Laotian Government forces, the Laotian Army armed several of its T-6s and used them as close-support aircraft. Belgium made similar use of its Harvards of the Kamina Flying School in the Congo in the early nineteen-sixties.

Since first entering service with the RCAF more than twenty-five years ago, a total of 15,495 T-6/SNJ/Harvards have been built. They have trained hundreds of thousands of fliers in more than forty countries and, though they are slowly being replaced in many of the world's air forces, still rank as the world's most widely used training aircraft. The following pages contain a selection of photographs representative of the T-6s far-flung foreign service career.

Harvard IIB's of the Royal Belgian Air Force. (Photo: Royal Belgian Air Force; the Nagtegaal Collection)

Heavily-armed T-6s of the Brazilian Air Force flew coastal patrol missions during World War II.
(Photo: North American Aviation)

T-6G of the 2nd Liaison and Observation Squadron, Brazilian Air Force. A life raft is carried in the belly container. (Photo: J. R. de Mendonca)

T-6s of the "Esquadrilla de Fumaca" (Smoke Squadron"), the official aerobatic team of the Brazilian Air Force. (Photo: J. R. de Mendonca)

Emblem of the "Esquadrilla de Fumaca". (Photo: J. R. de Mendonca)

Brazilian T-6s on a formation training flight. (Photo: North American Aviation)

Harvard IIA of the Royal Danish Air Force. (Photo: Royal Danish Air Force; the Nagtegaal Collection)

Student boards T-6 of the Chinese Nationalist Air Force. (Photo: the Nagtegaal Collection)

T-6G of the French Air Force. (Photo: French Air Force; the Nagtegaal Collection)

Federal German Air Force Harvard Mk. IV. (Photo: Federal German Air Force; the Nagtegaal Collection)

Federal German Air Force Harvard Mk. IV. (Photo: the Menard Collection)

T-6 of the Royal Hellenic Air Force. (Photo: Royal Hellenic Air Force; the Nagtegaal Collection)

Harvard IIA of the Royal Netherlands Air Force lifts from the runway. (Photo: Royal Netherlands Air Force; the Nagtegaal Collection)

Harvard IIA of the Dutch Civil Flying School. (Photo: the Nagtegaal Collection)

Harvard IIA of the Royal Netherlands Air Force. (Photo: Royal Netherlands Air Force; the Nagtegaal Collection)

The Harvard aerobatic team of the Dutch Government Civil Flying School won the European International formation aerobatic competitions of 1947, 1948, and 1949. The aircraft were flown by instructors. Above: a close-up view of the leader. Below: the leader and his two wingmen are roped together! (Photo: the Nagtegaal Collection)

Imperial Iranian Air Force T-6G with provision for armament. (Photo: the Nagtegaal Collection)

Harvard Mk. IV of the Italian Air Force. (Photo: Italian Air Force; the Nagtegaal Collection)

T-6 of the Italian Air Force. (Photo: Italian Air Force; the Nagtegaal Collection)

Italian Air Force T-6 on an air-to-air photography flight. (Photo: Italian Air Force; the Nagtegaal Collection)

T-6F of the Japanese Air Self-Defense Force. (Photo: the Menard Collection)

Above and below: Harvard IIAs of the Royal New Zealand Air Force. (Photos: Royal New Zealand Air Force; the Nagtegaal Collection) Opposite: Harvard Mk. IIIs of the Portuguese Air Force. (Photo: Portuguese Air Force; the Nagtegaal Collection)

1607
1622

Harvard IIAs of the Royal Rhodesian Air Force. (Photo: Royal Rhodesian Air Force; the Nagtegaal Collection)

Harvard IIA of the Swiss Air Force. (Photo: Swiss Air Force; the Nagtegaal Collection)

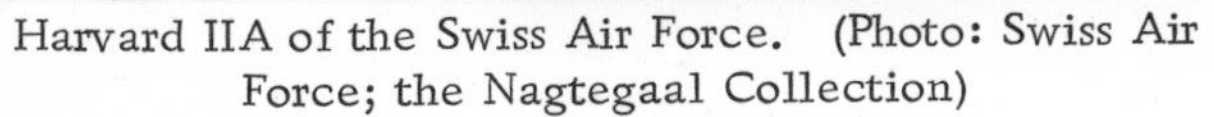
Harvard IIA of the Swiss Air Force. (Photo: Swiss Air Force; the Nagtegaal Collection)

T-6 of the Spanish Air Force. (Photo: Spanish Air Force; the Nagtegaal Collection)

T-6 for Thailland, fresh from the line at North American. (Photo: North American Aviation)

Harvards of the Operational Training School of the South African Air Force. (Photo: South African Air Force; the Nagtegaal Collection)

The aircraft illustrated on these two pages are all of the South African Air Force. The current South African aircraft nationality marking is shown in the photograph above. (Photos: South African Air Force; the Nagtegaal Collection)

7458
7458

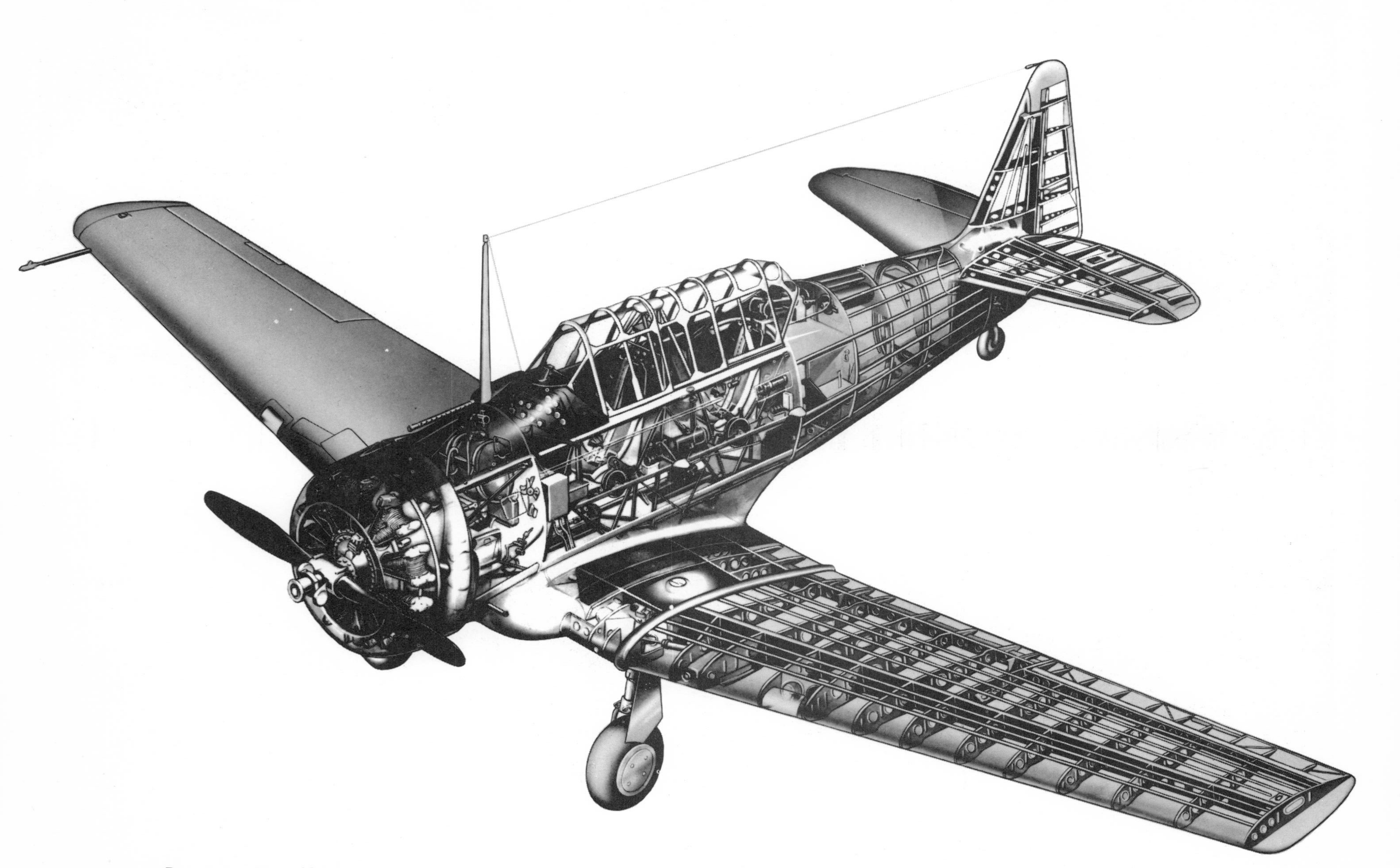

— Drawing courtesy North American Aviation.

AT-6D. (Photo: North American Aviation)

SNJ-4. (Photo: North American Aviation)

STANDARD SPECIFICATION

NORTH AMERICAN AVIATION
AT—6 ADVANCED TRAINER

TYPE: Two-place advanced training monoplane.

WINGS: Low-wing full cantilever monoplane, consisting of one two-spar center section and two removable single spar outer panels with detachable wing tips. Split type trailing edge flaps between ailerons. Wing spars and ribs of aluminum alloy construction.

FUSELAGE: The fuselage structure from the firewall to the rear cockpit is of chrome-molybdenum steel tube construction with welded steel fittings. The section from the rear cockpit to the tail is of aluminum alloy semi-monocoque construction. The side panels of the forward section are of aluminum alloy construction and are removable.

TAIL UNIT: Tail surface frames are of aluminum alloy construction. Horizontal and vertical stabilizers are covered with aluminum coated aluminum alloy. Elevator and rudder are smooth, flush type and fabric covered. Quick opening inspection doors are provided. The horizontal stabilizer is full cantilever and non-adjustable. Balanced type elevator equipped with tabs for longitudinally trimming the airplane in flight. The vertical stabilizer is full cantilever and non-adjustable. Rudder is balanced type equipped with trim tab for directional trim in flight.

UNDERCARRIAGE: Main landing gear is retractable cantilever single leg half fork type supported at the front spar of the center section. Wheels retract upward toward center line of ship hydraulically by means of an engine driven hydraulic pump. Steerable tail wheel swivels 360° with any degree of shock absorber inflation.

POWER PLANT: One 550 h.p. Pratt and Whitney "Wasp" model R-1340-AN-1 radial, air-cooled engine. Hamilton Standard model 12-D-40 controllable pitch, constant speed, two-bladed propeller. Oil system arranged to form an integral part of the engine section unit, in order that it will be removable when disconnecting the engine mount from the firewall. Fuel tanks in wing center section of welded aluminum construction with a service capacity of 111 gallons.

ACCOMMODATION: Two tandem cockpits under one enclosure with individually operated sliding panels for ingress and egress of the crew. Complete dual flight and engine controls are provided in each cockpit.

DIMENSIONS: Span, 42' 1/4"; length, 28' 11-7/8"; height, 11' 8-33/64"; wing area, 253.72 sq. ft.; tail group area, 63.43 sq. ft.

WEIGHTS AND LOADINGS: Weight empty, 4,158 lbs.; useful load, 1,142 lbs.; gross weight, 5,300 lbs.; wing loading, 20.7 lbs. per sq. ft.; power loading, 9.5 lbs. B.H.P.

ARMAMENT: One .30 fixed machine gun on the right hand side of the fuselage forward of the pilot's cockpit, one .30 fixed machine gun in the leading edge of the right hand outer wing panel, and one .30 machine gun mounted flexibly in the rear cockpit.

PERFORMANCE: Maximum speed at 5,000 feet, 205 m.p.h.; operating speed at 5,000 feet, 170 m.p.h.; landing speed, 67 m.p.h. Range, 750 miles; service ceiling, 21,500 feet.

The following pages contain a reprint of the main body of the AT-6 manual. Certain performance charts and technical data have been eliminated in the interests of space.

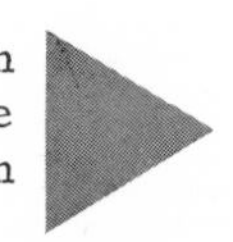

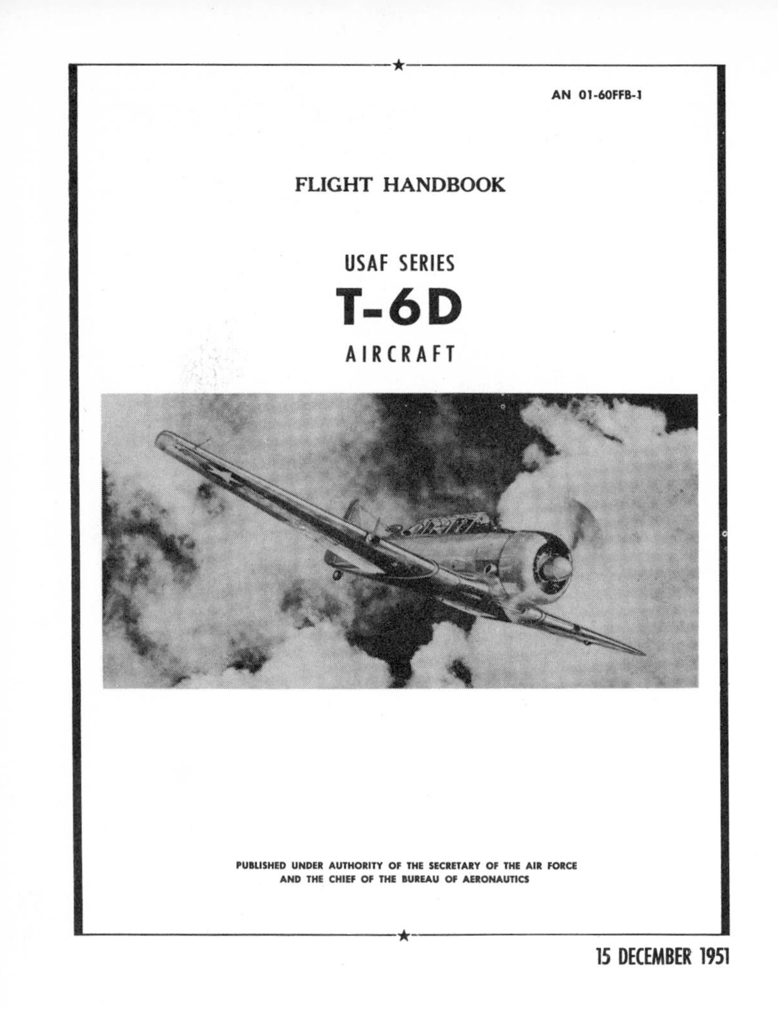

AN 01-60FFB-1

FLIGHT HANDBOOK

USAF SERIES

T-6D

AIRCRAFT

PUBLISHED UNDER AUTHORITY OF THE SECRETARY OF THE AIR FORCE
AND THE CHIEF OF THE BUREAU OF AERONAUTICS

15 DECEMBER 1951

Figure 1-1. T-6D Airplane

DESCRIPTION

SECTION I

AIRPLANE.

Few airplanes in this country are more familiar to military pilots than the T-6. In addition to training our own Air Force, Navy, and Marine pilots in precision flying, the T-6 is used in the Air Forces of a majority of the United Nations. More than 15,000 of the T-6 Series Airplanes have been built, and most of them are still in active service.

The T-6 (formerly the AT-6), which is designated the SNJ by the Navy and is known by a host of other names in the Air Forces of the world, is an outgrowth of the NA-16, the prototype of the entire series of famed training planes. The NA-16 was the first airplane designed and built by North American Aviation. It took off from Logan Field at Dundalk, Maryland, in 1934 after being designed and built in less than 9 weeks.

The T-6D, the fourth in the T-6 series, is essentially the same airplane as the original T-6. Its career began in 1940 when the first model rolled off the North American assembly lines. Known as the "Texan," it helped teach thousands of American and Allied pilots their flying ABC's during World War II. Today, the T-6 is still in the forefront of training pilots to defend America. Its flying, maintenance, and training qualities have proved so impressive that 11 years after it was first built, the T-6 is still teaching men throughout the world to fly a military airplane. The airplane is a two-place, dual-controlled, single-engine trainer. (See figure 1-2.) Solo flight is permitted only from the front cockpit because of restricted visibility from the rear seat and inadequate controls in the rear cockpit. On training flights, the student uses the front cockpit while the instructor occupies the rear, except for instrument training, during which the student occupies the rear seat. Provisions for armament—which consist of bombing equipment, a flexible gun in the rear cockpit, a wing gun, and a cowl gun—are incorporated in all airplanes. The airplane also incorporates a steerable tail wheel.

AIRPLANE DIMENSIONS.

Approximate over-all dimensions of the airplane are:

- Length .... 29.0 feet
- Wing span .... 42.0 feet
- Height (to top of rudder in level-flight attitude) .... 12.0 feet

AIRPLANE GROSS WEIGHT.

The normal weight of the airplane, with full fuel tanks, is approximately 5250 pounds. Maximum gross weight is approximately 6000 pounds, which includes both pilots, externally mounted bombs, and maximum permissible load in baggage compartment.

MAIN DIFFERENCES TABLE.

The main differences between the T-6D Airplane and the T-6G Airplane are outlined in the following table:

ITEM	T-6D	T-6G
Fuel Capacity	110 US. gallons	140 US. gallons
Electronics	AN/ARC-3, AN/AIC-2, AN/ARN-7, RC-193A	SCR-522A, Contractor-designed interphone (part of SCR-522A), complete provisions for AN/ARN-5A and RC-103A
Rear Cockpit Instruments	Flight instruments only are identical to those in front cockpit	Full complement of instruments identical to those in front cockpit, except hydraulic pressure gage
Armament	Two fixed forward-firing .30-caliber guns, bombing equipment, one flexible .30-caliber gun (provisions)	None
Hydraulic System	Actuated by power control lever in either cockpit	Actuated automatically by gear or flap control handle
Oxygen Equipment	High-pressure oxygen system (early airplanes), low-pressure (demand) system (late airplanes)	None

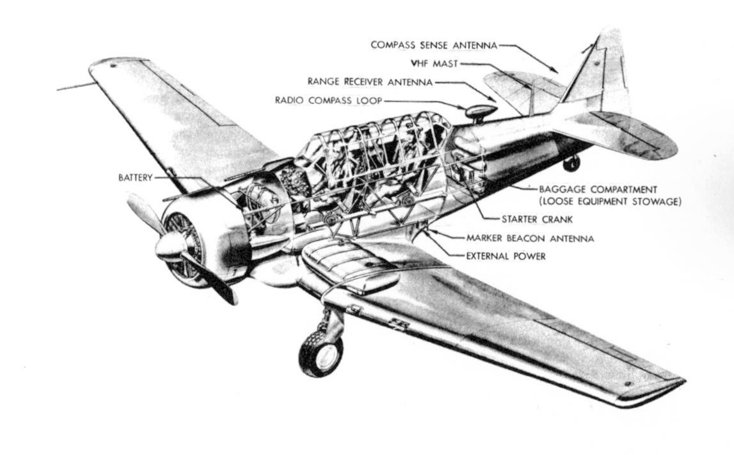

Figure 1-2. General Arrangement

1. Clock
2. Spare Lamp
3. Altimeter
4. Suction Gage
5. Airspeed Indicator
6. Magnetic Compass
7. Turn-and-Bank Indicator
8. Directional Gyro
9. Spare Lamp
10. Rate-of-Climb Indicator
11. Gyro Horizon
12. Engine Gage Unit
13. Cylinder Head Temperature Gage
14. Carburetor Mixture Temperature Gage
15. Fuel Switch-over Signal Light
16. Manifold Pressure Gage
17. Tachometer
18. Accelerometer
19. Recognition Light Switches
20. Radio Compass Indicator
21. Marker Beacon Signal Light
22. Instrument Subpanel
23. Ignition Switch

Figure 1-3. Front Cockpit—Forward View

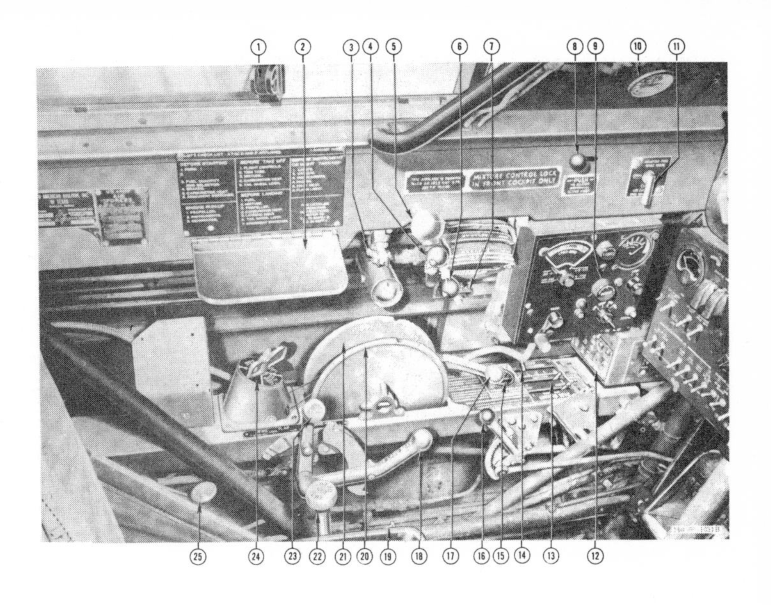

1. Canopy Handle
2. Armrest
3. Cockpit Light Control Knob
4. Mixture Control
5. Throttle
6. Propeller Control
7. Throttle Quadrant Friction Lock
8. Instrument Flying Hood Release Handle
9. Radio Compass Control Panel
10. Free Air Temperature Gage
11. Manifold Pressure Gage Drain Valve Handle
12. Circuit Breakers
13. Landing Gear Position Indicators
14. Wing Flap Position Indicator
15. Hydraulic Pressure Gage
16. Carburetor Air Control
17. Hand Fuel Pump Handle
18. Landing Gear Handle
19. Shoulder Harness Lock Handle
20. Elevator Trim Tab Control Wheel
21. Rudder Trim Tab Control Wheel
22. Hydraulic Hand-pump Handle
23. Wing Flap Handle
24. Fuel Selector
25. Hydraulic Power Control Lever

Figure 1-4. Front Cockpit—Left Side

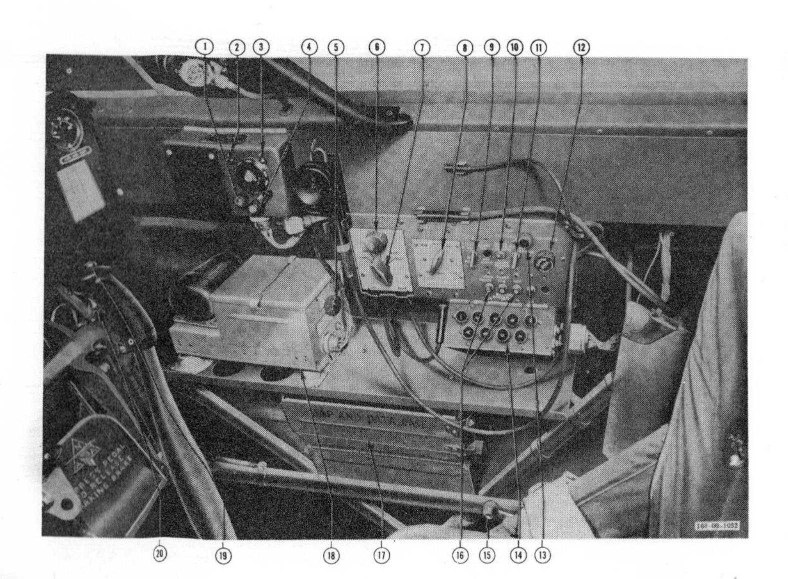

1. Range Receiver Volume Control
2. Range Receiver AB Switch
3. Range Receiver Power Switch
4. Range Receiver Tuning Crank
5. Interphone Amplifier Altitude Compensation Switch
6. Master Volume Control Knob
7. Master Selector Switch
8. Radio Range Filter Switch
9. VHF Audio Switch
10. Range-Volume Switch
11. VHF Control Transfer Switch
12. VHF Audio Control Knob
13. VHF Control Indicator Light
14. VHF Channel Selector Buttons
15. Seat Adjustment Lever
16. Circuit Breakers
17. Map and Data Case
18. Interphone Amplifier
19. Bomb Release Button
20. Gun Trigger

Figure 1-5. Front Cockpit—Right Side

Figure 1-6. Instrument Subpanel

ENGINE.

The airplane is powered by a 550-horsepower, nine-cylinder Pratt & Whitney radial engine, Model R-1340-AN-1. The engine is equipped with an updraft float-type carburetor and a direct-cranking starter.

ENGINE CONTROLS.

Throttle and mixture controls are located on the throttle quadrant on the left side of each cockpit. A friction lock (7, figure 1-4) on the inboard face of the quadrant in the front cockpit only is rotated to increase friction of the throttle, mixture, and propeller controls. Carburetor mixture temperature is controlled by a carburetor air control in the front cockpit.

THROTTLE. A throttle (5, figures 1-4 and 1-9) is located on the quadrant on the left side of each cockpit. A take-off stop is provided in the quadrant so that the pilot can feel when he has reached Take-off Power, at sea level. (See figure 1-7.) The throttle in the front cockpit can be pushed through the stop to obtain full throttle travel when additional power is needed at altitudes above sea level.

Figure 1-7. Throttle Quadrant

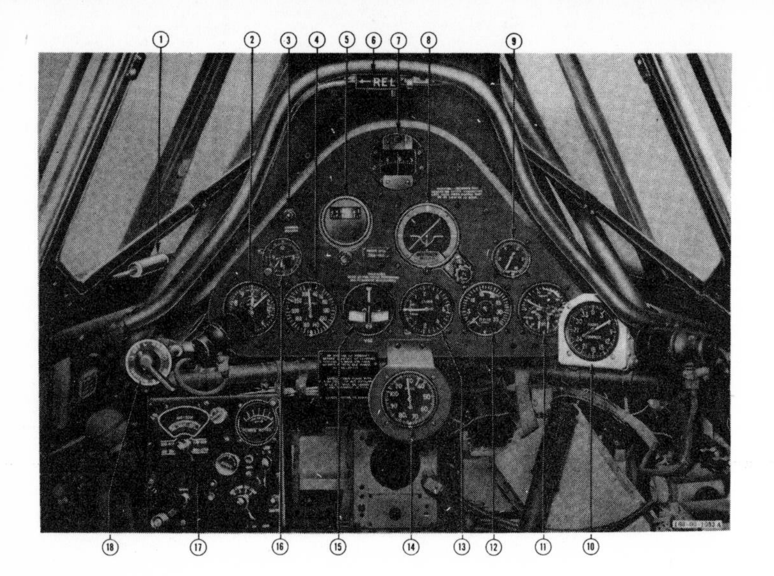

1. Canopy Handle
2. Altimeter
3. Marker Beacon Signal Light
4. Airspeed Indicator
5. Directional Gyro
6. Instrument Flying Hood Latch
7. Magnetic Compass
8. Gyro Horizon
9. Suction Gage
10. Radio Compass Indicator
11. Engine Gage Unit
12. Tachometer
13. Rate-of-Climb Indicator
14. Manifold Pressure Gage
15. Turn-and-Bank Indicator
16. Clock
17. Radio Compass Control Panel
18. Ignition Switch

Figure 1-8. Rear Cockpit—Forward View

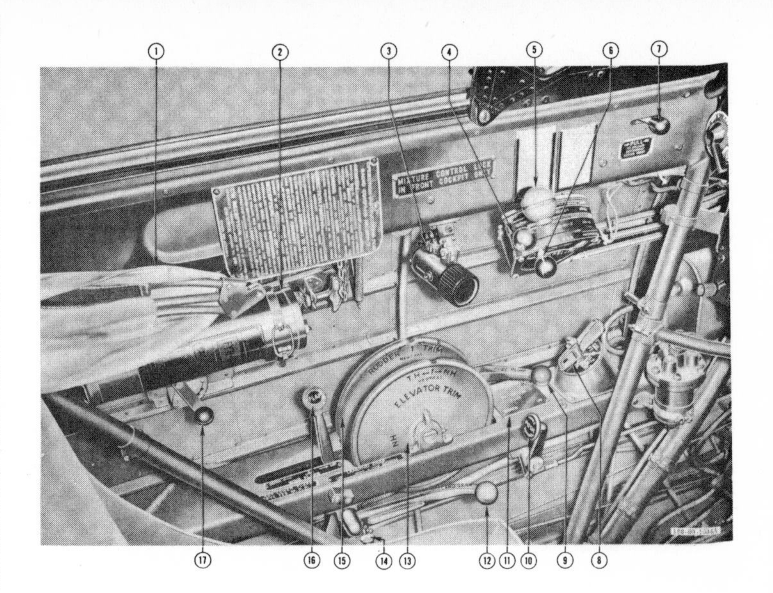

1. Instrument Flying Hood
2. Fire Extinguisher
3. Cockpit Light Control Knob
4. Mixture Control
5. Throttle
6. Propeller Control
7. Instrument Flying Hood Release Handle
8. Fuel Selector
9. Hand Fuel Pump Handle
10. Hydraulic Power Control Lever
11. Wing Flap Position Indicator (Some Airplanes)
12. Landing Gear Handle
13. Elevator Trim Tab Control Wheel
14. Shoulder Harness Lock Handle
15. Rudder Trim Tab Control Wheel
16. Wing Flap Handle
17. Ventilating-air Handle

Figure 1-9. Rear Cockpit—Left Side

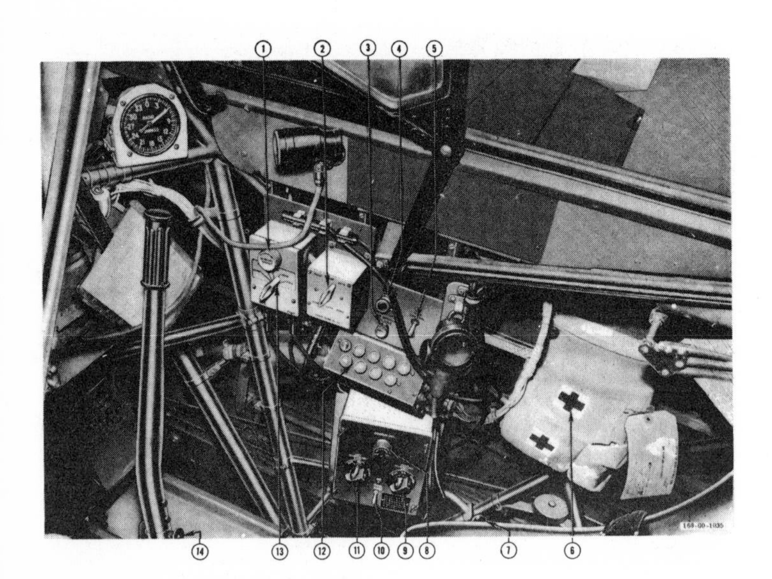

1. Master Volume Control Knob
2. Radio Range Filter Switch
3. Range Receiver Volume Control
4. VHF Control Indicator Light
5. VHF Control Transfer Switch
6. First-aid Kit
7. Seat Adjustment Lever
8. Compass Light Rheostat
9. Fluorescent Light Rheostat
10. Fuel Quantity Gage Light Switch
11. Fluorescent Light Rheostat
12. VHF Channel Selector Buttons
13. Master Selector Switch
14. Control Stick Release Knob

Figure 1-10. Rear Cockpit—Right Side

1. Parking Brake Handle
2. Rudder Pedal Adjustment Levers
3. Engine Primer
4. Hot-air Temperature Control Valve
5. Cold-air Temperature Control Valve
6. Control Lock Handle
7. Oil Cooler Shutter Control

Figure 1-11. Front Cockpit—Controls

MIXTURE CONTROL. The mixture control (4, figures 1-4 and 1-9) on the throttle quadrant in each cockpit enables the pilot to control the fuel-air mixture to the engine, to obtain efficient engine operation and maximum fuel economy. Positions on the quadrant are RICH (full forward) and LEAN (aft—idle cutoff). Any position between RICH and LEAN is in the manual leaning range. (See figure 1-7.) The front cockpit mixture control is equipped with a spring-loaded lock and ratchet. When the mixture control in either cockpit is moved forward, the lock is automatically released. However, before the mixture control can be moved aft toward LEAN, the lock must be released by pressing forward on the lock lever. The idle cutoff position shuts off all fuel flow at the carburetor to stop the engine.

CARBURETOR AIR CONTROL. The carburetor air control handle (16, figure 1-4) is located on the left console of the front cockpit. When the control is at COLD, ram air is admitted to the carburetor through the ram-air inlet on the left side of the engine cowl. (See figure 1-12.) As the control is moved toward the HOT position, it gradually closes the ram-air inlet while opening a duct that allows warm air from inside a muff surrounding the exhaust collector ring to mix with the cold ram air before being delivered to the carburetor. When the control is at the full HOT position, the ram-air inlet is fully closed and hot air only is drawn into the carburetor. The ram-air inlet is fitted with a filter. A carburetor mixture temperature gage (14, figure 1-3), mounted on the instrument panel in the front cockpit, indicates the temperature of the fuel-air mixture as it enters the engine.

IGNITION SWITCH. A standard ignition switch (23, figure 1-3; 18, figure 1-8) is located on the left side of the instrument panel in the front cockpit and forward of the throttle quadrant in the rear cockpit. Switch positions are OFF, L, R, and BOTH. The L and R positions are provided to check engine operation on the left or right magneto individually.

STARTER SWITCH. A guarded, toggle-type switch (figure 1-6), located on the front instrument subpanel, provides control of the starter. Originally the airplane was delivered with the starter wired to be energized by one switch and engaged (after coming up to speed) by another switch. However, the starter has been wired for direct cranking, so the switch marked "ENERGIZE" is inoperative. The switch marked "ENGAGE" will both energize and engage the starter to the engine. Power for energizing the starter can be derived from the airplane battery, although an external power source should be connected for this purpose, whenever possible, to conserve battery life.

ENGINE PRIMER. The engine priming system is controlled by a push-pull hand primer (3, figure 1-11) located below the instrument panel in the front cockpit. The primer pumps fuel from the hand fuel pump outlet directly into the five top cylinders to aid in starting. When not in use, the pump should be pushed in and turned to the right to the locked-closed position.

ENGINE CRANK.

An engine crank, stowed in the baggage compartment, is provided for emergency use to hand-crank the starter when electrical power is not available.

ENGINE INDICATORS.

A complete set of engine instruments is mounted in the front cockpit. The oil pressure, fuel pressure, and manifold pressure gages indicate pressure directly from the engine. When the engine is inoperative, the manifold pressure gage reading should correspond to barometric pressure. The tachometer and cylinder head temperature gage readings are self-generated and therefore do not require power from the electrical system of the airplane. Oil temperature and carburetor mixture temperature gages, however, depend upon the 28-volt d-c system. The engine gage unit (containing the oil temperature, oil pressure, and fuel pressure gages) and the tachometer are duplicated on the rear cockpit instrument panel. A manifold pressure gage is also installed in the rear cockpit of some airplanes.

MANIFOLD PRESSURE GAGE DRAIN VALVE.

A manifold pressure gage drain valve is provided to clear the manifold pressure instrument lines of moisture and vapors so that accurate indications can be obtained on the gage. The drain valve is opened on some airplanes by turning a handle (11, figure 1-4) located forward of the front cockpit throttle. On other airplanes, the drain valve is opened by depressing a button adjacent to the front cockpit manifold pressure gage. The differential between atmospheric pressure and manifold pressure enables flow through the instrument lines to clear them of vapors when the drain valve is opened. The valve should be opened only when the engine is operating below 30 inches manifold pressure so that the vapors will be carried into the engine instead of toward the gage. Also, a greater differential between atmospheric and manifold pressures exists at low power than at full power.

PROPELLER.

The engine drives a two-bladed, constant-speed, all-metal propeller. A propeller control is provided to select an engine rpm that is desired to be held constant. For information concerning propeller operation, refer to Section VII and see figure 7-2. The airplanes were originally delivered with a spinner covering the propeller hub, but most of the spinners have since been removed during service.

PROPELLER CONTROL. Engine rpm is determined by the setting of a propeller control (6, figures 1-4 and 1-9) located on the throttle quadrant in each cockpit. The propeller control may be placed at any intermediate position between DECREASE and INCREASE rpm, depending upon the engine rpm desired. Positioning the propeller control mechanically adjusts the setting of a propeller governor mounted on the nose section of the engine. The propeller governor maintains the selected rpm, regardless of varying air loads or flight attitudes. To enable maximum rated horsepower to be obtained for take-off, the propeller control is positioned to full INCREASE rpm. During a landing, the propeller control is set to obtain 2000 rpm to ensure immediate availability of power in case a go-around becomes necessary.

OIL SYSTEM.

Oil for engine lubrication is supplied from a 10.8-gallon tank. See figure 1-21 for oil specification and grade. Lubrication is accomplished by a pressure system with a dry sump and scavenge pump return. Oil flows from the tank to the engine pressure pump, which forces it through the engine, and is pumped back to the tank by the scavenge pump either directly or through the oil cooler, depending upon the temperature of the oil. The oil temperature is regulated by a thermostatic valve in the oil cooler which automatically controls the flow of oil through the cooler. Most airplanes incorporate a surge valve in the return line to enable oil to by-pass the cooler, preventing flow stoppage in case the oil congeals in the cooler.

OIL SYSTEM CONTROLS.

OIL COOLER SHUTTER CONTROL. The airplane is equipped with an oil cooler, which is located at the bottom of the engine mount. Oil cooler shutters, provided on the top side of the cooler, can be adjusted from the front cockpit only. The oil cooler shutter control (7, figure 1-11) is located in the front cockpit, below the instrument subpanel just forward of the control stick. The shutter control can be set at OPEN, CLOSED, or various intermediate positions to regulate the flow of air through the oil cooler.

OIL DILUTION SWITCH. An oil dilution system is provided for diluting the oil with gasoline before engine shutdown whenever a cold-weather start is anticipated. The oil dilution switch (figure 1-6), located on the instrument subpanel in the front cockpit, is spring-loaded to the OFF position and must be held ON to dilute the oil. When the switch is held in the ON position, fuel from the carburetor (under pressure) is allowed to enter the oil line to the engine to lower the viscosity of the oil.

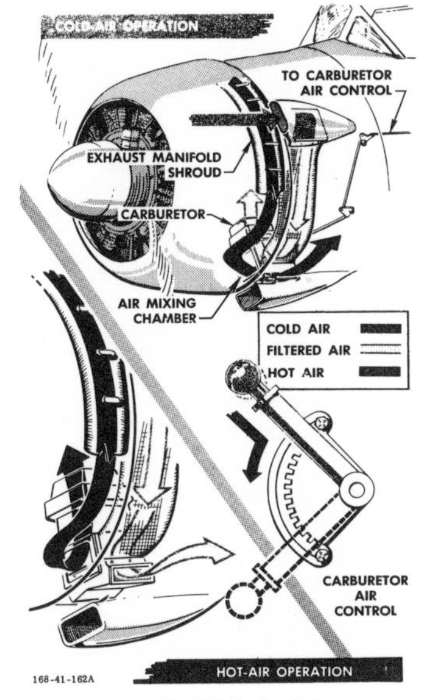

Figure 1-12. Air Induction System

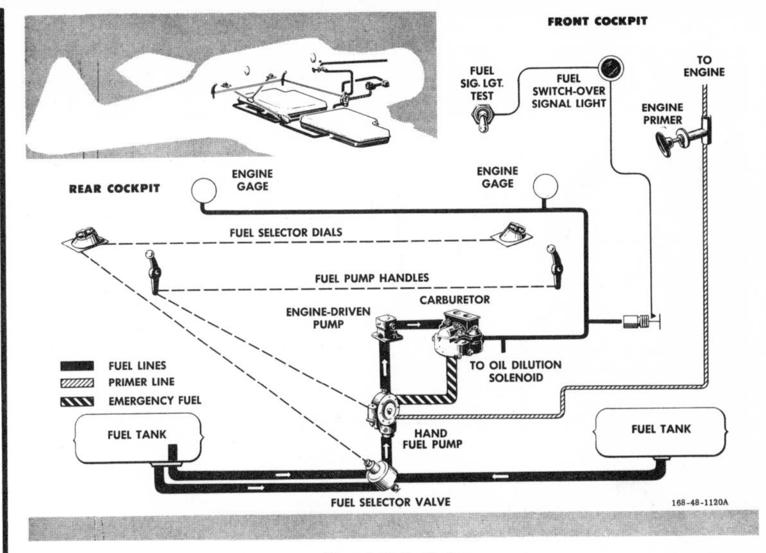

Figure 1-13. Fuel System

FUEL SYSTEM.

The fuel system (figure 1-13) incorporates two all-metal fuel tanks, which are located in the center section of the wing. See figure 1-14 for fuel quantity data. A fuel outlet with an extended standpipe is installed in the left tank to provide a 20-gallon reserve fuel supply. However, under certain conditions (figure 7-1), maneuvering flight can result in a reduction of the available reserve to a quantity as low as 10 gallons. Each tank sump is constructed so as to trap fuel around the tank outlets during inverted-flight maneuvers. An engine-driven fuel pump supplies fuel under pressure to the carburetor. In event of failure of the engine-driven pump, sufficient fuel pressure can be supplied to the carburetor by means of a hand fuel pump to enable full-power engine operation. Fuel flow by gravity is available only to the fuel selector valve and hand fuel pump. See figure 1-21 for fuel grade and specification.

FUEL SYSTEM CONTROLS.

FUEL SELECTOR. Selection of fuel supply is controlled by a fuel selector (24, figure 1-4; 8, figure 1-9) located on the left console of each cockpit. Both selector handles are interconnected. The positions of the selector are 20 GAL. RES., 35.2 GAL. LEFT, 55.2 GAL. RIGHT, and OFF. Each position has a detent to provide a distinct stop. When the selector is at 55.2 GAL. RIGHT, all the fuel in that tank may be used; with the selector at 35.2 GAL. LEFT, fuel will be consumed until the level of the extended standpipe is reached. The approximately 20 gallons remaining may be used only when the selector is placed at 20 GAL. RES. The OFF position is used to shut off all fuel flow.

HAND FUEL PUMP. A hand fuel pump, operated by interconnected handles (17, figure 1-4; 9, figure 1-9) located on the left console in each cockpit, will maintain fuel pressure in the event of an engine-driven fuel pump failure.

FUEL SYSTEM INDICATORS.

FUEL QUANTITY GAGES. A float-type fuel quantity gage (figure 1-15) is located on each side of the pilot's seat in the front cockpit. The gages are visible from the rear cockpit seat, with approximately a 5-gallon increase because of parallax error. The fuel gages

FUEL QUANTITY DATA
US. GALLONS

TANKS	NO.	FULLY SERVICED	USABLE FUEL IN LEVEL FLIGHT	EXPANSION SPACE	TANK VOLUME
L WING TANK	1	55.2	54.8	1.7	56.9
R WING TANK	1	55.2	54.8	1.7	56.9
TOTAL	2	110.4	109.6	3.4	113.8

NOTE:
Multiply gallons by 6.0 to obtain pounds gasoline (MIL-F-5572).
Estimated data shown in red.

168-48-1121

Figure 1-14. Fuel Quantity Data

are not sufficiently accurate for exact readings; therefore, the values should be regarded as approximate. The left gage reading includes the amount in reserve, so when the quantity indicated approaches (RES) 20 gallons, the selector should be moved from the 35.2 GAL. LEFT position; otherwise, engine failure from lack of fuel will result.

FUEL PRESSURE GAGE. Fuel pressure is indicated on the engine gage unit (12, figure 1-3; 11, figure 1-8). The fuel pressure gage is the direct-reading type and indicates fuel pressure in the carburetor.

FUEL SWITCH-OVER SIGNAL LIGHT. A signal light (15, figure 1-3) on the right side of the front cockpit instrument panel will illuminate when the fuel pressure drops below 3 psi. Should the fuel flow stop completely, as during a pump failure or in a restricted line, the light will illuminate approximately 10 seconds before the engine stops. A fuel signal light test switch (figure 1-6) is located on the instrument subpanel.

ELECTRICAL POWER SUPPLY SYSTEM.

Electrical power is supplied by a 50-ampere, engine-driven generator through a 28-volt, direct-current system. (See figure 1-16.) A 24-volt battery serves as a stand-by power source for use when the generator is inoperative or not supplying sufficient voltage. A reverse-current relay is incorporated to automatically control the generator. The generator "cuts in" at approximately 1250 rpm and "cuts out" when engine speed is reduced to approximately 1000 rpm. Full rated output of the generator is developed above 1650 rpm. Two inverters change direct current to alternating current to power the radio compass and remote-indicating compass.

CIRCUIT BREAKERS AND FUSES. All d-c circuits are protected from overloads by push-to-reset circuit breakers. The panel mounting the circuit breakers (12, figure 1-4) is located in the front cockpit on the left forward console. The communication equipment is protected by circuit breakers (12, figure 1-4; 16, figure 1-5) located in the front cockpit on the left and right side. Fuses are used to protect the communication equipment on early airplanes.

EXTERNAL POWER RECEPTACLE. An external power receptacle is located on the lower left side of the fuselage near the wing trailing edge. External power should always be used for engine starting or electrical ground checks whenever available, to conserve battery life for use during in-flight emergencies.

ELECTRICAL POWER SUPPLY SYSTEM CONTROLS AND INDICATOR.

BATTERY-DISCONNECT SWITCH. A battery-disconnect switch (figure 1-6) is located on the instrument subpanel. All electrical equipment is inoperative when the switch is OFF unless the generator is operating or an external power supply is connected to the airplane. The battery will supply current to all electrical equipment when the battery switch is ON and no other power source is being used. The switch should be OFF when the engine is not running, to prevent unnecessary discharge of the battery.

GENERATOR MAIN LINE SWITCH. A generator main line switch (figure 1-6), located on the instrument subpanel, provides a means of turning off the generator circuit in case the reverse-current relay fails to operate. The switch should be left ON at all times except in an emergency.

AMMETER. An ammeter (figure 1-6), located on the instrument subpanel, indicates the amount of current being delivered by the generator.

168-51-551A

FUEL QUANTITY GAGES ARE LOCATED ON EACH SIDE OF THE FRONT COCKPIT SEAT.

Figure 1-15. Fuel Quantity Gages

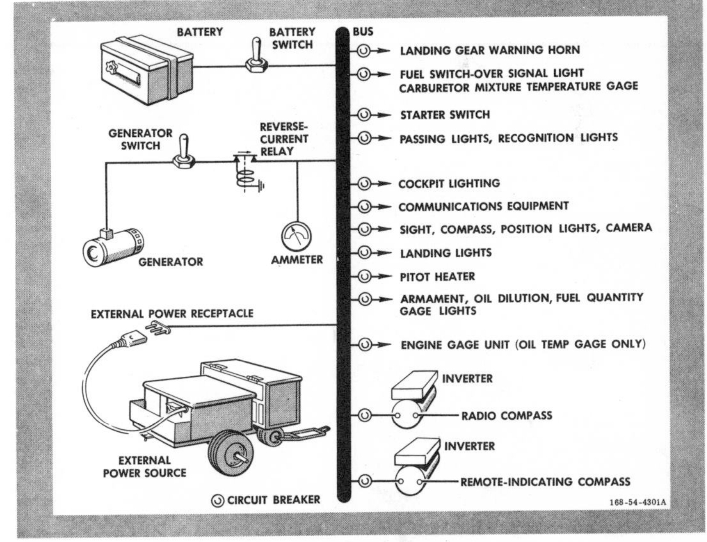

Figure 1-16. Electrical System

HYDRAULIC POWER SUPPLY SYSTEM.

The hydraulic system (figure 1-17) is utilized to operate the landing gear and flaps. An engine-driven pump supplies hydraulic pressure for operation of these units. However, when no hydraulic units are being operated in flight, the entire output of the pump is diverted to the reservoir. The hydraulic pressure gage (15, figure 1-4), located on the left console in the front cockpit, indicates pressure only when a unit is being operated. For hydraulic fluid grade and specification, see figure 1-21.

HYDRAULIC POWER SUPPLY SYSTEM CONTROLS.

POWER CONTROL LEVER. Hydraulic pressure is controlled by a power control lever (25, figure 1-4; 10, figure 1-9), located on the side of the left console in each cockpit. When the power control lever is depressed, with the engine-driven pump operating, hydraulic pressure is available to operate the landing gear and flaps. The power control lever operates on a time-lag principle and automatically disengages after a set length of time, which is approximately twice that necessary to operate the flaps and landing gear. After the power control lever disengages, fluid is diverted back to the reservoir.

HYDRAULIC HAND-PUMP. A hand-pump, incorporating a spring-loaded extension handle (22, figure 1-4), is located to the left of the pilot's seat in the front cockpit. The hand-pump is provided for emergency operation of the landing gear and flaps. When the engine-driven pump is in operation, the power control lever must be disengaged before the hand-pump will build up pressure; otherwise, system hydraulic pressure will impose a force in opposition to the hand-pump.

FLIGHT CONTROL SYSTEM.

The primary flight control surfaces (ailerons, rudder, and elevator) may be operated from either cockpit by conventional stick and rudder pedal controls. Rudder pedals, which are also used to apply the brakes and for tail wheel steering, are adjustable fore and aft. Trim tabs on the elevator and rudder are mechanically operated from either cockpit. Aileron trim tabs are adjustable on the ground only. The rudder pedals and control

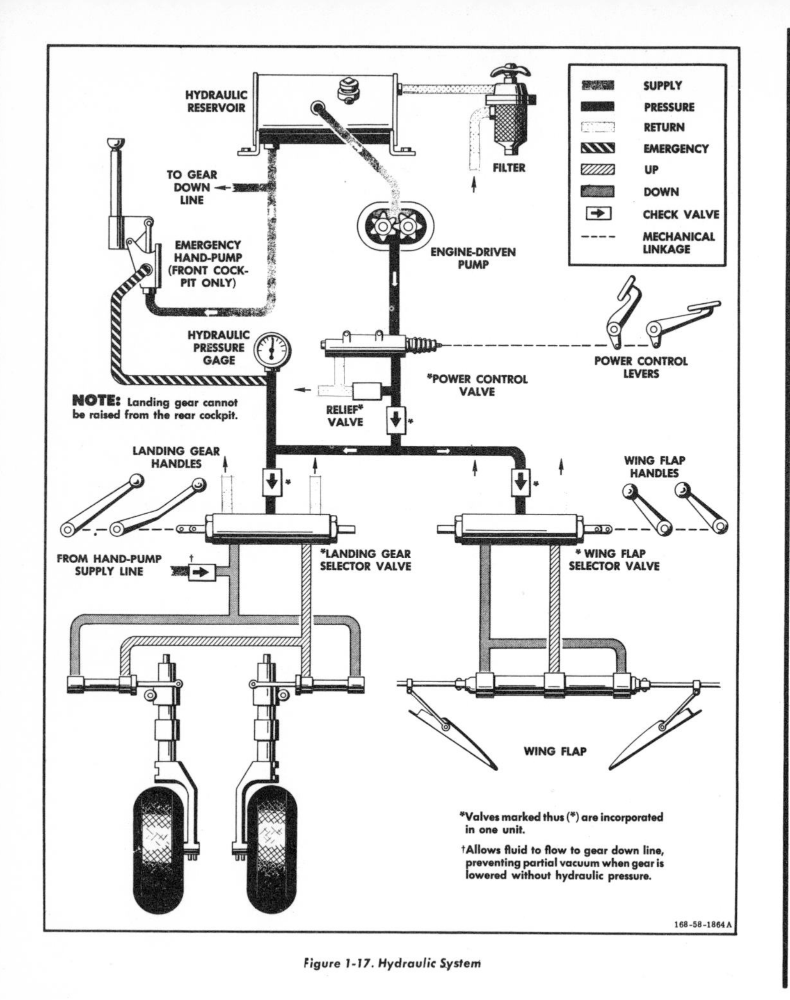

Figure 1-17. Hydraulic System

stick can be locked by a mechanical lock in the front cockpit.

FLIGHT CONTROLS.

CONTROL STICK. The control stick grip in the front cockpit incorporates a gun trigger and a bomb release button. The rear cockpit control stick, which can be stowed in a bracket at the left side of the cockpit, is removed by actuating a release knob (14, figure 1-10) at the lower rear side of the stick. In addition to conventional use of the control stick (for ailerons and elevators), it also unlocks the tail wheel (to free-swiveling) when placed full forward.

RUDDER PEDAL ADJUSTMENT. A rudder pedal adjustment lever (2, figure 1-11) is located on the inboard side of each rudder pedal in both cockpits. Adjustment of the pedals is accomplished by moving the individual rudder pedal lever inboard and adjusting the rudder pedal until the desired position is obtained. The lever is then released to lock the pedal in the selected position.

TRIM TAB CONTROLS. Rudder and elevator trim tab control wheels (20 and 21, figure 1-4; 13 and 15, figure 1-9) are located on the left console of each cockpit. Trim tab position may be determined from a pointer at each control wheel.

CONTROL LOCK HANDLE (AILERONS, RUDDER, AND ELEVATOR).

All surface controls are locked by means of a control lock handle (6, figure 1-11) located forward of the control stick in the front cockpit. In order for the controls to be locked, the rudder pedals must be in neutral and the stick forward of center. After the lock handle is raised from the forward (stowed) position, the control stick is moved into the lock recess and the handle is depressed rearward. When not in use, the lock should be stowed (full forward and down).

WING FLAPS.

Hydraulically operated, split-type wing flaps extend from aileron to aileron. The flaps, operable from either cockpit, travel 45 degrees to the full down position. The hydraulic system power control lever must be actuated in conjunction with the flap handle to operate the flaps.

WING FLAP HANDLE.

The wing flaps are operated by means of a control handle (23, figure 1-4; 16, figure 1-9), located on the left side of each cockpit. The flap control handle has three positions: UP, DOWN, and LOCKED. The LOCKED position is used only to lock the flaps in an intermediate position. The flaps are held in the respective up, down, or intermediate positions by trapped fluid in the lines.

WING FLAP POSITION INDICATOR.

A mechanical wing flap position indicator (14, figure 1-4) is located forward of the front cockpit trim tab control wheels. In some airplanes, a locally manufactured mechanical wing flap position indicator (11, figure 1-9) is provided in the rear cockpit behind the fuel selector.

LANDING GEAR SYSTEM.

The retractable main landing gear is hydraulically operated, and mechanical locks hold the gear in both the down and up positions. The locks are mechanically released by initial movement of the landing gear handle. In order to operate the gear, the hydraulic system power control lever must be engaged when the gear handle is actuated. In case of hydraulic failure, the gear can be unlocked by the landing gear handle and will extend by its own weight. The downlock pins will then snap in place. A means is provided to mechanically engage the downlock pins in an emergency. A plastic window (figure 1-18) on each wing, above the respective strut, makes possible a visual check of the downlock pin engagement. The tail wheel does not retract.

LANDING GEAR HANDLE.

The landing gear handle (18, figure 1-4; 12, figure 1-9) is mounted on the left console of each cockpit. The

GEAR EXTENDING (GEAR HANDLE DOWN). DOWNLOCK PIN IN EXTENDED POSITION.

GEAR DOWN BUT UNSAFE. DOWNLOCK PIN NOT ENGAGED.

GEAR FULLY DOWN WITH DOWNLOCK PIN PROPERLY ENGAGED.

Figure 1-18. Landing Gear Downlock Pin Engagement

handle in the front cockpit has three positions: UP, DOWN, and EMERGENCY. The EMERGENCY position is used to manually force the downlock pins into place should the pins fail to automatically lock the gear down. However, the handle must never be positioned to EMERGENCY *before* the gear is completely down; otherwise, the downlock pins, while manually forced into place, may not allow the gear to extend fully. The EMERGENCY position is reached by moving the handle to the extreme end of the sector, past a detent at the DOWN position. There is no neutral position, so the handle must remain in the selected position. The landing gear handle in the rear cockpit has an UP and a DOWN position, but will only extend the gear. Although the rear handle can be raised, it will not cause the gear to retract, because the front handle is engaged in a detent when at DOWN. (See figure 1-19.)

Do not operate the front cockpit landing gear handle when the airplane is on the ground, as there is no safety provision to prevent retraction of the gear.

LANDING GEAR INDICATORS.

LANDING GEAR POSITION INDICATOR. A mechanical landing gear position indicator (13, figure 1-4), is located on the left forward console of the front cockpit. The indicator shows the approximate position of each gear at all times.

LANDING GEAR DOWNLOCK INDICATOR LIGHTS. Locally manufactured downlock indicator lights (figure 4-2), on the leading edge of each wing near the wheel well, are incorporated on some airplanes. Although these indicator lights are not visible to the pilot, they enable ground-observer verification of gear position as a safety feature for night flight training.

LANDING GEAR WARNING HORN. A warning horn is located in the overturn structure above the rear instrument panel. If the landing gear is not locked in

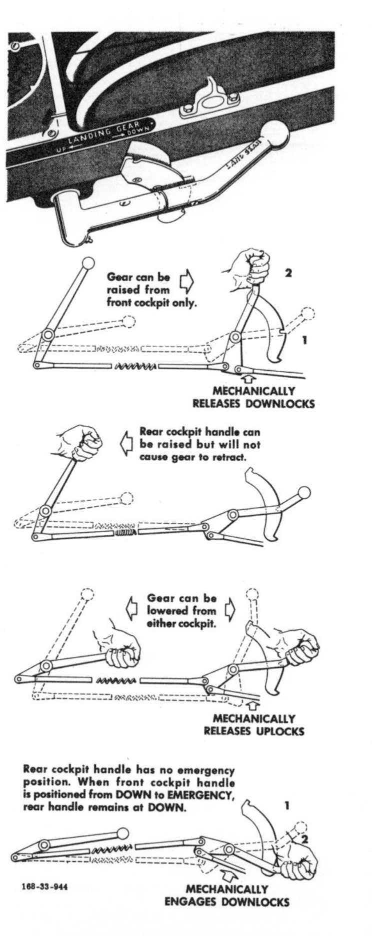

Figure 1-19. Landing Gear Handle

the down position, the horn will blow when the throttle is retarded.

STEERING SYSTEM.

The nonretractable tail wheel can be steered or allowed to free-swivel, as determined by the position of the control stick. With the control stick in any position except full forward, the tail wheel can be steered by the rudder pedals up to a maximum of 15 degrees either side of center. Moving the control stick to the full forward position allows the tail wheel to free-swivel, and the airplane must be steered by the brakes. If the tail wheel is not aligned with the rudder when the control stick is moved back from the full forward position, the wheel will not be controllable. However, subsequent alignment with the rudder will automatically engage the tail wheel for steering.

BRAKE SYSTEM.

Hydraulic brakes on the main wheels are operated by

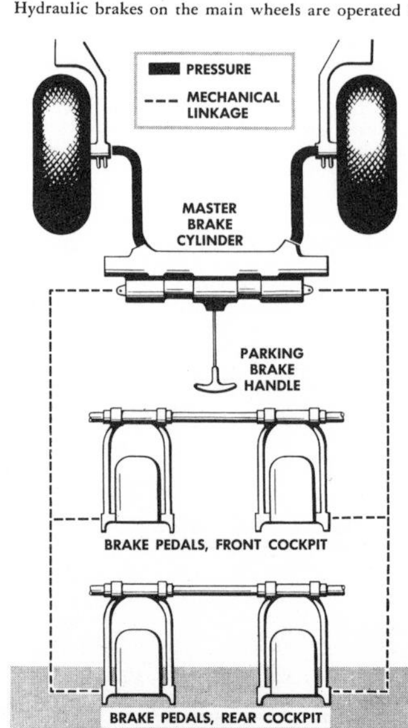

Figure 1-20. Brake Hydraulic System

application of toe pressure on the rudder pedals. No emergency method of applying the brakes is provided. The brake system (figure 1-20) incorporates a master brake cylinder with an integral reservoir. A parking brake handle (1, figure 1-11) is installed in the front cockpit. Parking brakes are set by depressing the toe brakes, pulling the parking brake handle out, and then releasing the toe brakes. The parking brakes are released by depressing the toe brakes in either cockpit. See figure 1-21 for grade and specification of brake fluid.

INSTRUMENTS.

A complete set of engine and flight instruments is installed in the front cockpit. The rear cockpit is equipped with duplicate flight instruments for instrument flight training purposes, but the tachometer and engine gage unit are the only engine instruments installed. A manifold pressure gage is also installed in the rear cockpit of some airplanes. A suction gage is provided in each cockpit. The gyro horizon, directional gyro, and turn-and-bank indicator are operated by the engine-driven vacuum system. The airspeed indicator, altimeter, and rate-of-climb indicator are operated by the pitot-static system. This system measures the difference between impact air pressure entering the pitot tube, mounted on the right wing, and static air pressure obtained at vent ports in the side of the pitot head. The airspeed indicator is connected to both the impact and static lines of the system. The altimeter and rate-of-climb indicator are connected to the static ports only. To keep the pitot tube opening clean, a cover is placed over the pitot head whenever the airplane is parked. An accelerometer (18, figure 1-3) is installed in the front cockpit below the instrument panel in some airplanes. The free air temperature gage (10, figure 1-4) is installed either in the windshield near the top or on the left side of the front cockpit.

EMERGENCY EQUIPMENT.

HAND-OPERATED FIRE EXTINGUISHER.

A carbon tetrachloride fire extinguisher (2, figure 1-9) is installed on the left side of the rear cockpit. The extinguisher can also be reached from outside the cockpit through an access door above the wing trailing edge.

FIRST-AID KIT.

A first-aid kit (6, figure 1-10), installed on the right side of the rear cockpit, is provided for emergency use.

CANOPY.

The canopy has two sliding sections, one over each cockpit, which are controlled separately by handles on the exterior and interior. The front sliding section can be locked at four positions: open, closed, and two intermediate positions. The rear sliding section can be locked at three positions: open, closed, and an intermediate position. Both side panels on each sliding section can be forcibly pushed out free from the canopy to provide an emergency exit from the airplane. Each side panel incorporates an emergency release handle (figure 3-5) which is safetied by fine wire to prevent accidental release.

SEATS.

The seats are adjusted by means of a seat adjustment lever (15, figure 1-5; 7, figure 1-10) at the right side of each seat. Pulling the lever back allows the seat to be raised or lowered. When the lever is pulled, the occupant is assisted in raising the seat by a bungee cord which tends to pull the seat up. A seat cushion is provided in each seat.

SHOULDER HARNESS LOCK HANDLE. A two-position (locked and unlocked) shoulder harness lock handle (19, figure 1-4; 14, figure 1-9) is located on the left side of each seat. A latch is provided for positively retaining the handle at either position of the quadrant. When the top of the handle is pressed down, the latch is released and the handle may be moved freely from one position to another. The shoulder harness will lock automatically when you lean full back in the seat, provided the lock handle is forward and the harness is adjusted for proper fit. The shoulder harness should be locked for all take-offs and landings (crash or otherwise) and during acrobatics.

Before a forced landing, all switches not readily accessible with the harness locked should be "cut" before the harness lock handle is moved forward to the locked position.

AUXILIARY EQUIPMENT.

Section IV contains all information pertaining to the description and operation of auxiliary equipment. Included in Section IV are the heating and ventilating systems, communication and associated electronic equipment, lighting equipment, oxygen system, armament equipment, and miscellaneous equipment.

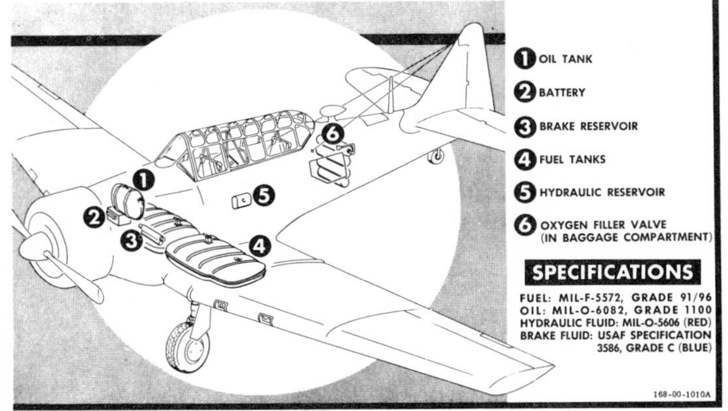

Figure 1-21. Servicing Diagram

NORMAL PROCEDURES

SECTION II

BEFORE ENTERING THE AIRPLANE.

FLIGHT RESTRICTIONS.

Detailed airplane and engine limitations are listed in Section V.

PREFLIGHT PLANNING.

From the operating data contained in the Appendix, determine fuel consumption, correct airspeed, and power settings as necessary to accomplish the intended mission. The Appendix data will enable you to properly plan your flight so that you can obtain the best possible performance from the airplane.

WEIGHT AND BALANCE.

Refer to Section V for weight and balance limitations. Refer to Handbook of Weight and Balance Data (AN 01-1B-40) for loading. Before each mission, make the following checks:

1. Check take-off and anticipated landing gross weight and balance.
2. Make sure fuel, oil, armament, and special equipment carried are sufficient for the mission to be accomplished.
3. Make sure weight and balance clearance (Form F) is satisfactory.

EXTERIOR INSPECTION.

Make an exterior inspection, starting at the front cockpit and going clockwise around the airplane. See figure 2-1 for complete inspection procedure.

Note

The cockpits are accessible from the left side of the airplane only. To open canopy, pull up on canopy handle, and slide front cockpit section aft and rear cockpit section forward.

ON ENTERING THE AIRPLANE.

INTERIOR CHECK (ALL FLIGHTS).

Make the following checks before starting the engine:

1. Check rear cockpit for presence of first-aid kit.
2. Fill out Form 1.
3. Unlock flight controls and check for free movement with correct response.
4. Fasten safety belt and shoulder harness. Check operation of shoulder harness lock.
5. Adjust seat and rudder pedals.
6. Set parking brakes.
7. Adjust headset.
8. Check fuel quantity gages. Fuel selector 20 GAL. RES.

Note

Steps for starting engine and subsequent ground operation include checking all positions of fuel selector.

9. Check that hydraulic hand-pump handle is not extended.

Starting at the front cockpit, make the following checks:

During this preflight check, inspect entire exterior for wrinkles, loose rivets, dents, and loose access doors.

1 COCKPIT

Ignition and battery-disconnect switches ***OFF.***
Gun safety switch ***SAFE.***
Check form 1.
Verify that airplane has been serviced with required quantities of fuel, oil, hydraulic fluid, and oxygen.
Oil and hydraulic reservoir caps secure.
Controls locked and trim tabs neutral.
Wing flap handle and indicator up.
If flying solo, rear cockpit control stick stowed and safety belt, shoulder harness, oxygen equipment, microphone, headset, and canopy secured.

2 LEFT WING

Visually check fuel quantity.
Check wing flaps for full up position.
Aileron and trim tab neutral and hinges secure.
Condition of position lights and wing tip.

3 LEFT LANDING GEAR

Condition of landing light, downlock light, torque linkage, and uplock.
Wheel chocked.
Extension of gear strut (1 to 2 inches).
Tire for proper inflation, condition, and slippage.
Hydraulic leaks.

4 POWER PLANT SECTION

Propeller free of nicks and oil leaks.
Cowling secure and free of foreign objects.
Carburetor air and oil cooler scoops clear.

5 RIGHT LANDING GEAR

Same as opposite side.

6 RIGHT WING

Same as opposite side.
Pitot head cover removed.

7 FUSELAGE RIGHT SIDE

Condition of fuselage lights.

8 EMPENNAGE

Rudder, elevators, and respective trim tabs neutral, and hinges secure.
Condition of position lights.
Extension of tail wheel strut (approx 6 in. from top of tire to bottom of fuselage).
Tire for proper inflation, condition, and slippage.
Grounding wire secure.

9 FUSELAGE LEFT SIDE

Baggage and loose equipment secured if carried.
Baggage compartment locked closed.
Fire extinguisher serviceable.

Figure 2-1. Exterior Inspection

10. Landing gear handle DOWN. Check gear position indicator.
11. Carburetor air control COLD.
12. Oil cooler shutter control OPEN.
13. Radio compass power switch OFF.
14. Manifold pressure drain valve handle CLOSED.
15. Check generator switch ON.
16. Check all remaining switches at OFF or SAFE.
17. Circuit breakers in.
18. Altimeter and clock set.
19. Gyros UNCAGED.

Note

The gyro instruments should be uncaged at all times except during maneuvers which exceed operating limits. If gyro horizon bar is not level after engine is started, cage and uncage the gyro 5 minutes before take-off.

20. Note manifold pressure reading (field barometric pressure), for subsequent use during engine power check.
21. Test oxygen equipment for operation and check pressure gage. Low-pressure system (400 psi) – high-pressure system (1800 psi).
22. Communications equipment off and related circuit breakers in.
23. Adjust cockpit air temperature control valves as desired.

INTERIOR CHECK (NIGHT FLIGHTS).

If night flying is anticipated, the following additional checks should be made:

1. Have external power source connected. To prevent unnecessary discharge of battery, leave battery-disconnect switch OFF unless external power is not available.
2. With the aid of outside observer, test operation of position, passing, recognition, and landing lights. Check that landing gear downlock lights are illuminated.

Do not leave landing, passing, or recognition lights on for more than 10 seconds when airplane is on the ground, as excess heat may seriously damage the light.

3. Check operation of cockpit (fluorescent and incandescent), fuel quantity gage, and compass lights.
4. Push to test and adjust intensity of all indicator and warning lights.
5. Check for reliable flashlight on board.

STARTING ENGINE.

Start the engine as follows:

1. Check that propeller has been pulled through at least two revolutions.
2. Post fire guard and check propeller clear.
3. Throttle open approximately ½ inch.
4. Mixture control full RICH.
5. Check propeller control full DECREASE.

Since engine is normally shut down with propeller at decrease rpm, it must be started with propeller in same position so that full oil pressure will be available for engine lubrication during starting.

6. Unlock and check primer for free movement.
7. Call "Switches On!"
8. Have external power source connected. To prevent unnecessary discharge of battery, leave battery-disconnect switch OFF unless external power is not available.
9. Call "Clear?" and wait for assurance from ground crew before actuating starter switch. After the propeller turns over about two revolutions, turn ignition switch to BOTH.
10. Operate primer with slow, even strokes until the engine starts firing. If necessary, continue priming until engine runs smoothly. Lock primer. Do not prime a hot engine.

Do not use the hand fuel pump when starting engine, as fire may occur if engine backfires.

11. As the engine starts, release starter switch.

Note

Should a backfire result, retard the throttle slightly. Do not pump the throttle.

12. Adjust throttle to obtain 500 to 600 rpm as quickly as possible.

Refer to Section III for instructions in case of fire during starting.

13. Check oil pressure; if gage does not indicate 40 psi within 30 seconds, stop the engine and investigate.

14. Have external power supply disconnected and turn battery-disconnect switch ON.

15. Check operation of pitot heater with aid of ground crew.

WARM-UP PROCEDURE.

1. As soon as oil pressure indicates 40 psi, move propeller control to full INCREASE.
2. Throttle adjusted to obtain the smoothest rpm between 1200 and 1400 for warm-up.
3. VHF radio turned to proper channel.
4. Fuel selector 55.2 GAL. RIGHT.
5. Check generator operation at approximately 1250 rpm and 1000 rpm.

GROUND TESTS.

While the engine is warming up, perform the tests outlined in figure 2-2.

TAXIING INSTRUCTIONS.

Primary controls for taxiing the airplane are the throttle, steerable tail wheel, and brakes. Coordinate these controls for easy taxiing. Observe the following instructions and precautions for taxiing:

Don't "jockey" the throttle; if you do, the resultant sudden acceleration and deceleration will decrease the life and reliability of the engine.

Hydraulic system—check as follows: lower flaps with emergency hand-pump; then depress power control lever and check hydraulic pressure gage for normal pressure; finally raise flaps (with system pressure) in increments to check **HOLD** position.

With manifold pressure below 30 in. Hg, open manifold pressure gage drain valve for 3 seconds.

Carburetor air control—check operation. Note drop in manifold pressure with increase in mixture temperature.

Instruments—check for readings in desired ranges.

Communications equipment—check operation.

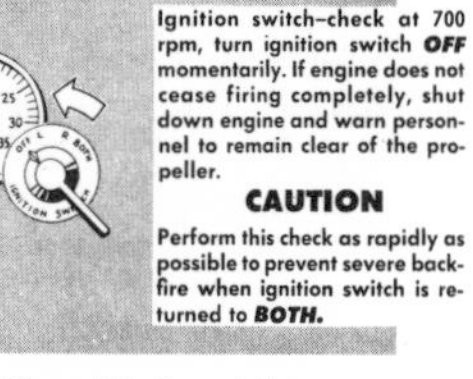

Ignition switch—check at 700 rpm, turn ignition switch **OFF** momentarily. If engine does not cease firing completely, shut down engine and warn personnel to remain clear of the propeller.

CAUTION

Perform this check as rapidly as possible to prevent severe backfire when ignition switch is returned to **BOTH.**

168-00-1036A

Figure 2-2. Ground Tests

1. Fuel selector 35.2 GAL. LEFT.
2. Have chocks pulled, allow airplane to roll forward slightly, and check the brakes.

Never allow taxi speed to build up before checking brakes.

3. The tail wheel, being steerable by use of the rudder pedals, provides ample control of the airplane under all normal taxiing conditions.

4. To make sharp turns, slow the airplane down, position control stick full forward to disengage tail wheel, and use the brakes to control the airplane. Never allow the inside wheel to stop during a turn. Turning with one wheel stopped may damage the wheel, tire, or strut.

5. The throttle is the main taxi speed control, and most taxiing can be accomplished with it in the closed or slightly open position. Brake usage should be kept to a minimum.

6. Tail wheel engaged. To engage the tail wheel for steering, the tail wheel and rudder must be aligned and the control stick must be back from full forward position. Alignment can be readily accomplished by allowing the airplane to roll forward slightly with the rudder neutral.

Note

Because of restricted forward visibility, S-turn the airplane well to both sides of the desired track to provide a clear, unrestricted view.

UPWIND TAXIING.

The stick should be held fully aft to hold the tail of the airplane on the ground and to ensure positive steering action of the tail wheel.

DOWNWIND TAXIING.

The stick should be held forward to keep the tail from lifting off the ground because of wind pressure being built up beneath the elevators.

Note

If the stick is *full* forward, the tail wheel will free-swivel.

CROSS-WIND TAXIING.

Hold stick into the wind to keep wings level. The primary means of airplane control will be by use of rudder, which is adequate even in extremely strong winds. If necessary, a slight amount of downwind brake may be used but should be held to a minimum.

BEFORE TAKE-OFF.

After taxiing to run-up position, face into the wind, hold brakes, and make the following airplane and engine checks.

PREFLIGHT AIRPLANE CHECK.

1. Primary controls:
   Check surface controls for free movement.
2. Instruments and Switches:
   Altimeter set.
   Directional gyro set.
   Gyro horizon set.
   All instrument readings in desired ranges.
   All switches at desired positions.
3. Fuel System:
   Fuel selector on proper tank (35.2 GAL. LEFT if airplane fully serviced, 55.2 GAL. RIGHT or 20 GAL. RES. if not). Refer to Section VII for instructions concerning fuel selection during flight.
   Mixture control full RICH.
   Primer locked.
4. Flaps:
   Flaps set for take-off (UP for normal take-off).
5. Trim:
   Trim tabs set for take-off (elevator—11 o'clock; rudder—2 o'clock).

PREFLIGHT ENGINE CHECK.

While performing checks requiring rpm reading, tap the instrument panel to prevent tachometer sticking.

1. Check propeller control at full INCREASE.
2. Propeller check — at 1600 rpm, pull propeller control back to full DECREASE position and note rpm drop of approximately 200 rpm; then return control to full INCREASE position.
3. Power check — adjust manifold pressure to field barometric pressure (as read on manifold pressure gage before starting engine) and check for 2000 (±50) rpm.

Note

If less than the prescribed rpm is obtainable for given manifold pressure, engine is not developing sufficient power and should be corrected before flight.

When running engine up to high power, be careful to have stick back and brakes applied.

4. Ignition system check — with throttle adjusted to 2000 rpm, position ignition switch to L and R and check for maximum drop of 100 rpm. The absence of *any* rpm drop indicates that the opposite magneto is not being electrically grounded during the test as it should be. Between checks, return ignition switch to BOTH to allow speed to stabilize. If drop exceeds 100 rpm, return ignition switch to BOTH and run engine up to Take-off Power for a few seconds to clear spark plugs; then recheck ignition system at 2000 rpm. Return ignition switch to BOTH at completion of test.

Note

During the test, observe the ring cowl for excessive vibration; a faulty ignition wire or one or more bad spark plugs will cause the cowl to vibrate excessively.

5. Idle speed check — with throttle against the idle stop, the engine should idle at 450 rpm.
6. Cruising fuel-air mixture check — with propeller control at full INCREASE and mixture control full RICH, allow engine speed to stabilize at 1800 rpm. Move mixture control into the manual leaning range until an approximate 100 rpm drop is noted; then return to RICH. The engine speed should increase very slightly before it decreases. An immediate decrease indicates the mixture is set too lean. A momentary increase in excess of 25 rpm indicates the mixture is set too rich.
7. Acceleration and deceleration check — with the mixture control at RICH, advance throttle from idle to 2000 rpm. Engine should accelerate and decelerate smoothly with no tendency to backfire.

Rapid reversal or sudden throttle movements must be avoided.

8. Oil cooler shutter control OPEN.
9. Carburetor air control full COLD.

TAKE-OFF.

Plan your take-off according to the following variables affecting take-off technique: gross weight, wind, outside air temperature, type of runway, and height and distance of the nearest obstacles. See figure A-4 for required take-off distances.

NORMAL TAKE-OFF.

In order to perform a take-off within the distance specified in the Take-off Distances (figure A-4), the following procedure must be used:

1. Visually check final approach for aircraft; then roll into take-off position and line up airplane with runway.
2. Shoulder harness LOCKED.
3. Canopy locked open for improved visibility and to permit immediate escape in case of sudden emergency.
4. Tail wheel engaged for steering.
5. Advance throttle smoothly to Take-off Power.
6. Raise the tail slightly after airplane has gained sufficient speed.
7. Allow the airplane to fly itself off the ground, using only slight back pressure on the control stick.
8. Normal take-off speed is approximately 80 mph.

Note

For procedure to follow if engine fails during take-off, refer to Section III.

MINIMUM-RUN TAKE-OFF.

A minimum-run take-off is a maximum performance maneuver with the airplane near stalling speed. It is directly related to slow flying and flaps-down stalls; consequently, you should be familiar with these maneuvers before attempting to make a minimum-run take-off. Complete all normal "before take-off" checks and follow the procedure outlined in figure 2-3 for a minimum-run take-off.

MINIMUM-RUN TAKE-OFF

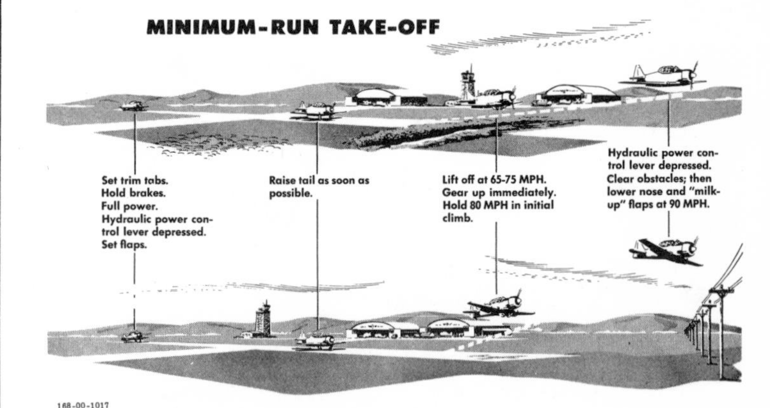

168-00-1017

Figure 2-3. Minimum-run Take-off Procedure

CROSS-WIND TAKE-OFF.

The following procedure is recommended for cross-wind take-off:

1. Advance throttle to Take-off Power setting and maintain directional control with rudder.
2. Continue as in a normal take-off, applying sufficient aileron pressure to maintain level attitude.
3. When airplane attains flying speed, apply sufficient stick pressure to make a positive break with the ground.
4. After becoming air-borne, counteract drift by making a coordinated turn into the wind.

NIGHT TAKE-OFF.

Night take-off procedure is the same as for daylight operation. However, a thorough knowledge of switch and light location is essential. The following additional checks are recommended for night take-off:

1. Turn cockpit lights low.
2. Tune radio carefully and loud, as it will fade during take-off and flight.
3. Hold airplane steady on a definite reference point during the take-off run.
4. Don't be alarmed by exhaust flame.

AFTER TAKE-OFF.

1. When the airplane is definitely air-borne, depress hydraulic power control lever and move landing gear handle to UP. Approximately 15 seconds is required for gear retraction.
2. Reduce engine output to Maximum Continuous Power by first retarding throttle, then propeller control.

Note

For training purposes, reduce power to 30 inches manifold pressure at 2000 rpm.

3. Establish a constant climb attitude.

CLIMB.

1. Advance throttle to maintain manifold pressure during climb.

Note

For training purposes, maintain 110 mph, 30 inches manifold pressure, and 2000 rpm.

2. Adjust oil cooler shutter control as necessary to maintain correct oil temperature.

3. Close canopy upon reaching 3000 feet, and lean mixture for smooth operation.

4. Refer to Normal Power Climb chart (figure A-5) for climb data power settings, recommended airspeed, rate of climb, and fuel consumption.

FLIGHT CHARACTERISTICS.

All data on flight characteristics is incorporated in Section VI.

SYSTEMS OPERATION.

Information pertaining to use of Take-off Power, manual leaning of carburetor mixture, propeller operation, carburetor icing, detonation, preignition, and fuel system operation is included in Section VII.

DESCENT.

Descending with throttle closed, gear and flaps up, long distances can be covered with a comparatively small loss of altitude. Lowering either the flaps or landing gear greatly steepens the gliding angle and increases the rate of descent. Before entering a descent, close throttle and move mixture control toward RICH to provide smooth engine operation at the reduced rpm. Because the engine cools rapidly during a descent with the throttle retarded, clear the engine approximately every half minute by advancing the throttle slowly and smoothly to 25 inches manifold pressure to prevent fouled plugs.

Do not allow cylinder head temperature to drop below 100°C during descent.

For training purposes, the following should be accomplished.

1. Open canopy as a safety precaution upon reaching 3000 feet.
2. Mixture control full RICH to prevent engine roughness and possible cutout during descent.

TRAFFIC PATTERN CHECK LIST.

Traffic pattern procedure and check list are shown in figure 2-4.

LANDING.

FINAL APPROACH AND TOUCHDOWN.

In order to obtain the results stated in the Landing Distances (figure A-6), accomplish the approach and landing procedures outlined in figure 2-4. In addition, observe the following precautions and techniques: Just before reaching end of runway, start flare. Use smooth, continuous back pressure on the stick to obtain a tail-low attitude for landing. Change attitude evenly and slowly; don't jerk the controls or go down in steps. Note that the attitude for this landing is similar to that attained in a gear- and flaps-down stall. Touch down in three-point attitude. The ailerons are only partially effective at low speeds but can still be used advantageously during the round-out and touchdown. Since the vertical stabilizer is offset to the left almost 2 degrees to counteract propeller torque at cruising speeds, a slight amount of left rudder pressure should be applied throughout the round-out and touchdown to prevent swerving to the right when landing in calm wind or straight into the wind. After touchdown, hold the stick back to help keep the tail down for positive tail wheel steering. Refer to Section III for information regarding emergency landings.

LANDING ROLL.

Since most landing accidents in this airplane occur during the landing roll, it is during this operation that you must be extremely alert. Immediately on touchdown, the airplane might swerve suddenly or skip on the runway. This sudden swerve is sometimes caused by landing in a slight drift or skid. Use ailerons, as necessary, to counteract a wing-low condition. Remain alert for a tendency to swerve to the right. When possible, take advantage of runway length to save brakes. Test brakes carefully before their use becomes a necessity and apply them soon enough to avoid abrupt braking action. Since the rudder, which is the main directional control, will be less effective as you slow down, you must be particularly alert as you near the end of the landing roll.

CROSS-WIND LANDING.

Use either the wing-low, crab, or combination method of landing in a cross wind.

1. Allow for drift while turning on final approach so that you won't overshoot or undershoot the approach leg.
2. Establish drift correction as soon as drift is detected.
3. Velocity and direction of the wind will determine the amount of flaps used for the landing.

Note

Since an airplane acts like a weather vane, it attempts to swing into the wind. Flaps increase this weather-vaning tendency, so use a minimum degree of flaps in a cross wind.

4. Use ailerons, as necessary, to counteract a wing-low condition during the round-out and touchdown.

NIGHT LANDING.

The same techniques and procedures used for day landings will be applied. Don't turn on the landing lights at too high an altitude and avoid using them at all if landing in fog, smoke, or thick haze, as reflection from

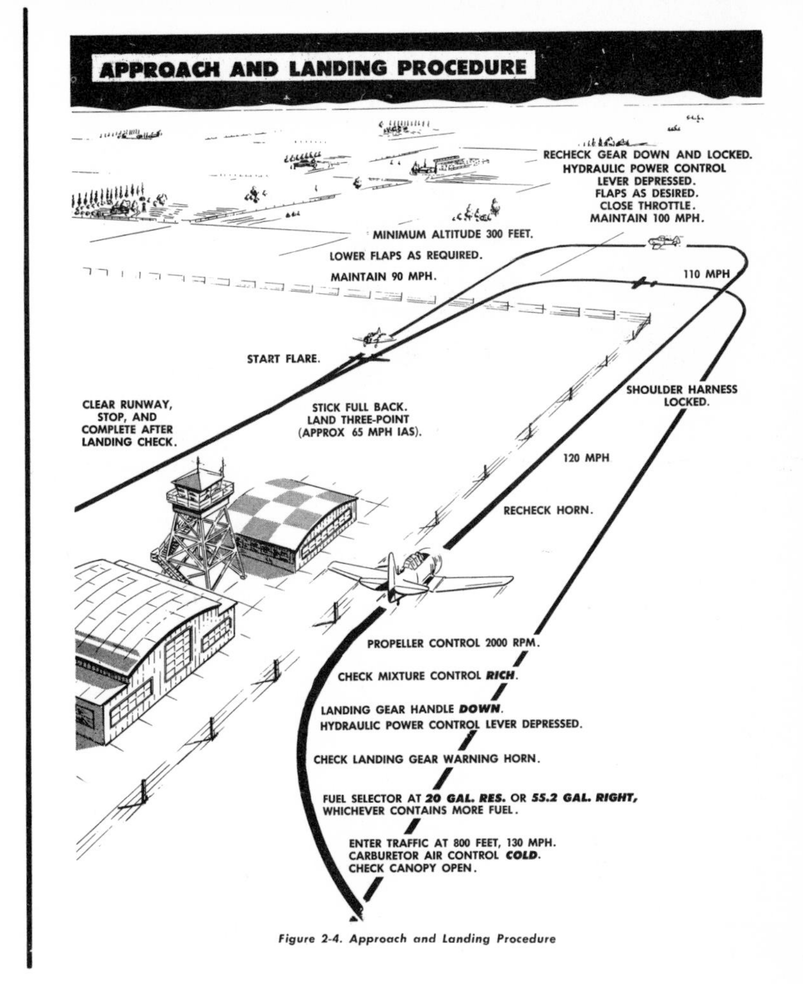

Figure 2-4. Approach and Landing Procedure

AT 90 MPH IAS AND ABOVE 200 FT, "MILK-UP" FLAPS.

CLEAR TRAFFIC.

RETRIM.

ADVANCE THROTTLE SMOOTHLY; DO NOT EXCEED 30 IN. Hg WITH 2000 RPM.

LANDING GEAR HANDLE UP.

Figure 2-5. Go-around

the lights impedes vision and may distort depth perception. Alternate the use of landing lights while taxiing after landing.

GO-AROUND.

A typical go-around procedure is shown in figure 2-5. Decide early in the approach whether it is necessary to go around and start before you reach too low an altitude.

AFTER LANDING.

After the landing roll, clear the runway immediately and come to a complete stop. Before taxiing to the line:

1. Wing flap control UP.
2. Trim tab controls neutral.
3. Propeller control full INCREASE.
4. Oil cooler shutter control OPEN.

POSTFLIGHT ENGINE CHECK.

After the last flight of the day, make the following checks:

Note

While performing checks requiring rpm reading, it may be necessary to tap the instrument panel to prevent tachometer sticking, especially in cold weather.

1. Check propeller control at full INCREASE.
2. Ignition switch check—at 700 rpm, turn ignition switch OFF momentarily. If engine does not cease firing completely, shut down engine and warn personnel to remain clear of the propeller until the ignition discrepancy has been corrected.

Perform this check as rapidly as possible to prevent severe backfire when ignition switch is returned to BOTH.

3. Idle speed and mixture check—with throttle against idle stop, the engine should idle at 450 rpm. When engine idle speed is stabilized, move the mixture control slowly and smoothly toward idle cutoff. Carefully observe the manifold pressure gage for any change during the leaning procedure. The manifold pressure should decrease slightly before it increases. An immediate increase indicates the mixture is set too lean. A momentary decrease in excess of 1/4 in. Hg indicates the mixture is set too rich. Return mixture control to RICH before engine cuts out.
4. Power check—adjust manifold pressure to field barometric pressure (as read on altimeter with elevation set to zero) and check for 2000 (±50) rpm.

Note

If less than the prescribed rpm is obtainable for given manifold pressure, engine is not developing sufficient power and should be corrected before the next flight.

When running engine up to high power, be careful to have stick back and brakes applied.

5. Cruising fuel-air mixture check—with propeller control at full INCREASE and mixture control full RICH, allow engine speed to stabilize at 1800 rpm. Move mixture control into the manual leaning range until an approximate 100 rpm drop is noted; then return to RICH. The engine speed should increase very slightly before it decreases. An immediate decrease indicates the mixture is set too lean. A momentary increase in excess of 25 rpm indicates the mixture is set too rich.
6. Ignition system check—with throttle adjusted to 2000 rpm, position ignition switch to L and R and check for rpm drop (not to exceed 100 rpm). Return ignition switch to BOTH between checks to allow speed to stabilize. If drop exceeds 100 rpm, return ignition switch to BOTH and run engine up to Take-off Power for a few seconds; then recheck ignition system at 2000 rpm. Return ignition switch to BOTH at completion of test.

Note

Any discrepancies detected during the postflight check should be entered on Form 1.

STOPPING ENGINE.

When a cold-weather start is anticipated, dilute oil as required by the lowest expected temperature. For oil dilution instructions, refer to Section IX.

1. Parking brakes set.
2. Open throttle to approximately 1500 rpm, place propeller control in full DECREASE, and allow engine to run for approximately one minute to allow the oil from the propeller to be scavenged back to the oil tank.
3. Stop engine by pulling mixture control full aft (idle cutoff).
4. When propeller stops, close throttle completely and turn ignition switch to OFF.
5. Radio off.
6. All electrical switches off.
7. Battery switch OFF. Leave the generator switch ON.
8. Fuel selector OFF.

BEFORE LEAVING AIRPLANE.

1. Have the wheels chocked; then release brakes.
2. Lock the surface controls.
3. Complete Form 1.
4. Close canopy.

EMERGENCY PROCEDURES

SECTION III

ENGINE FAILURE.

Engine failures fall into two main categories: those occurring instantly, and those with ample indication prior to failure. The instant failure is rare and usually occurs only if the ignition or fuel flow completely fails. Most engine failures are gradual and afford the alert pilot ample indication that he may expect a failure. An extremely rough-running engine, loss of oil pressure, excessive cylinder head temperature under normal flight conditions, loss of manifold pressure, and fluctuating rpm are indications that a failure is imminent. When indications point to an engine failure, the pilot should make a landing immediately.

PROCEDURE ON ENCOUNTERING PARTIAL ENGINE FAILURE.

Should engine failure appear imminent, and if altitude permits and it is reasonably safe to attempt to regain normal engine operation, proceed as follows:

1. Fuel selector to 55.2 GAL. RIGHT or 20 GAL. RES., depending on which tank contains more fuel.

Note

Fuel switch-over signal light will usually illuminate approximately 10 seconds prior to complete failure of engine if difficulty is caused by fuel starvation.

2. If necessary, maintain adequate fuel pressure with hand fuel pump.
3. Mixture control full RICH.
4. Propeller control full INCREASE.
5. Check ignition switch at BOTH.
6. Carburetor air control HOT, if icing conditions exist.

PROCEDURE ON ENCOUNTERING COMPLETE ENGINE FAILURE.

Should the engine fail completely, and if there is still sufficient altitude and it is reasonably safe to restart the engine, accomplish the foregoing procedure (partial engine failure) and then proceed as follows:

1. Move mixture control to idle cutoff.
2. Advance throttle to full OPEN for a few seconds to clear engine.
3. Readjust throttle to ½ inch open.
4. Mixture control full RICH.
5. Prime engine if necessary.

Should this procedure fail to restart the engine, shut down engine as follows:

1. Mixture control to idle cutoff.
2. Throttle CLOSED.
3. Ignition switch OFF.
4. Fuel selector OFF.
5. Battery and generator switches OFF except when power is desired to operate lights or communication equipment.

ENGINE FAILURE UNDER SPECIFIC CONDITIONS.

ENGINE FAILURE DURING TAKE-OFF. Should the engine fail during the take-off run, immediately close throttle and apply brakes. If remaining runway is insufficient for stopping and it becomes necessary, collapse the landing gear; then if time permits, move the mixture control to idle cutoff. Get clear of airplane immediately.

ENGINE FAILURE AFTER TAKE-OFF. If the engine fails immediately after take-off, proceed as follows:

1. Lower nose immediately to maintain airspeed above stall.
2. Landing gear handle UP. (Even if there is not sufficient time or hydraulic pressure to completely raise gear, it is better to have it unlocked so that it will collapse on landing. Judgment should be used on long runways where a gear-down landing could be accomplished.)
3. Fuel selector OFF.
4. Land straight ahead, changing direction only enough to miss obstacles. Don't try to turn back to the field—making a crash landing straight ahead with airplane under control is much better than turning back and taking the chance of an uncontrolled roll into the ground. (See figure 3-1.)

ENGINE FAILURE DURING FLIGHT. If the engine fails during flight:

1. Lower nose as speed drops, to maintain glide at approximately 95 mph.
2. If altitude permits, attempt to restart engine.

Do not attempt restart if engine stopped because of obvious mechanical failure.

3. If it is impossible to restart engine, make a forced landing if possible; otherwise, bail out.

MAXIMUM GLIDE. Maximum glide distance can be obtained by maintaining a speed of 95 mph with gear and flaps up and with propeller control at full DECREASE rpm to minimize drag. See figure 3-2, for optimum glide path. Glide ratio and rate of descent at best glide speed under varying conditions are as follows:

	MPH IAS	GLIDE RATIO	RATE OF DESCENT
Gear up, flaps up	95	9.6 to 1	857 fpm
Gear down, flaps up	85	7.5 to 1	966 fpm
Gear up, flaps down	75	7 to 1	930 fpm
Gear down, flaps down	70	6.1 to 1	1004 fpm

DEAD-ENGINE LANDING.

See figure 3-4 for procedure to follow in case of a forced landing (power off) with gear up or down.

Figure 3-1. Land Straight Ahead

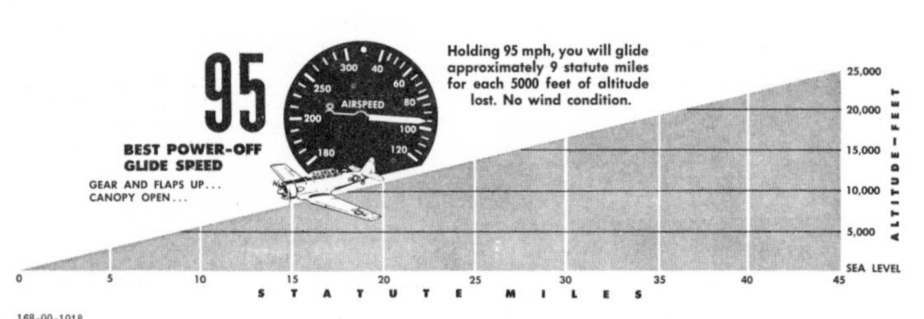

Figure 3-2. Maximum Glide

PROPELLER FAILURE.

A runaway condition of the propeller caused by excess power and decreased load on the engine can occur in a prolonged dive, and the engine may exceed the overspeed limit of 2800 rpm. At first evidence of a runaway or overspeeding propeller:

1. Retard throttle.
2. Adjust propeller control in an attempt to bring propeller within limits.
3. Pull airplane up in a climb to increase load on engine.

FIRE.

During starting, engine fire can occur in the induction system or in the exhaust system. However, pilot technique is the same in combating both types of fires. Should a fire occur in the engine accessory section, the engine should be stopped immediately.

Note

No fire extinguishing system is installed on this airplane.

ENGINE FIRE DURING STARTING.

1. Continue cranking in attempt to clear or start engine, as fire may be drawn through engine or blown out the exhaust stacks and extinguished. Do not prime engine again.
2. If engine does not start, continue cranking, mixture control to idle cutoff, and fuel selector, ignition, and generator switches OFF.
3. If fire continues, stop cranking and turn battery switch OFF.
4. Get clear of airplane and signal ground crew to use portable fire extinguishing equipment.

ENGINE FIRE AFTER STARTING.

1. Keep the engine running, as the fire may be drawn through the engine and extinguished.

2. If fire continues to burn, shut down engine.
3. Get clear of the airplane and signal the ground crew to use the portable fire equipment.
4. Do not restart the engine until the cause of the fire has been determined.

ENGINE FIRE DURING FLIGHT.

Depending upon the severity of the fire, either bail out immediately or shut down the engine as follows in an attempt to extinguish the fire:

1. Mixture control to idle cutoff.

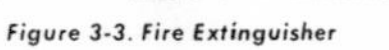

Figure 3-3. Fire Extinguisher

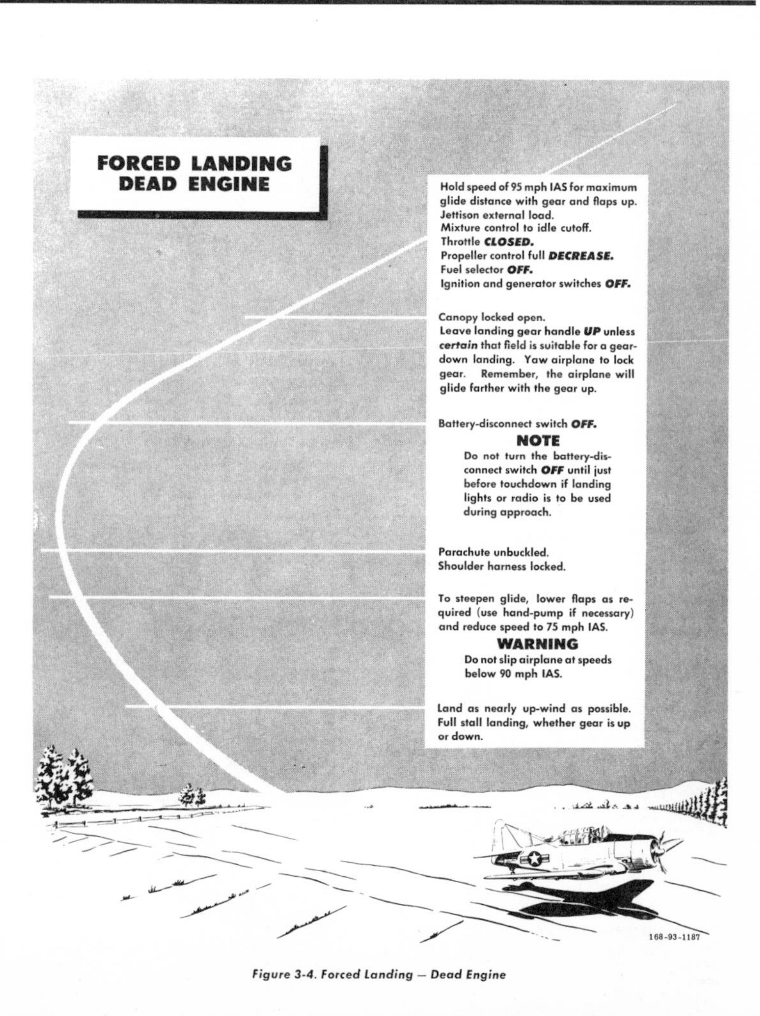

Figure 3-4. Forced Landing — Dead Engine

2. Throttle CLOSED.

3. Ignition switch OFF.

4. Fuel selector OFF.

5. Battery and generator switches OFF except when power is desired to operate lights or communication equipment.

FUSELAGE FIRE DURING FLIGHT.

1. Reduce airspeed immediately, in preparation for bail-out (if it becomes necessary) and to lessen possibility of fire spreading.

2. If smoke or fumes enter cockpit, use oxygen (if carried) or open canopy.

3. Generator and battery switches OFF.

4. If fire persists, shut down engine as outlined in the foregoing procedure.

5. If possible, use hand fire extinguisher (figure 3-3), located on left side of rear cockpit.

Toxic fumes can be generated where fire extinguisher fluid (carbon tetrachloride) contacts hot metal.

6. If fire is not extinguished immediately, bail out.

WING FIRE.

1. Turn off all wing light switches (position, passing, and landing), armament switches, and pitot heater switch.

2. Attempt to extinguish fire by sideslipping airplane away from flame.

3. If fire is not extinguished immediately, bail out.

ELECTRICAL FIRE.

Circuit breakers isolate most electrical circuits and automatically interrupt power to prevent a fire when a "short" occurs. If necessary, however, turn generator and battery switches OFF to remove power from all electrical equipment and land as soon as possible. If electrical power is essential, as during instrument flight, an attempt to identify and isolate the shorted circuit may be feasible. This can be accomplished as follows:

1. With generator and battery switches OFF, turn off all remaining switches (except ignition, of course).

2. Turn generator switch ON. If generator circuit is shorted, return switch to OFF and place battery switch ON instead.

3. Individually turn each circuit on again, allowing a short period of time before proceeding to the next, until the shorted circuit is identified.

SMOKE ELIMINATION.

Should smoke or fumes enter the cockpit, proceed as follows:

1. Reduce airspeed immediately, in preparation for bail-out (if it becomes necessary) and to minimize spreading of fire.

2. Open cold-air outlets.

3. Use oxygen (if carried) or open canopy.

LANDING EMERGENCIES.

GEAR RETRACTED.

If the gear fails to extend, a wheels-up landing can be made on either hard or soft ground as follows:

1. Establish a normal flaps-down approach.

2. Flare out as in a normal landing (with tail low) This will enable tail wheel to absorb the initial shock.

3. Mixture control to idle cutoff.

4. Get clear of airplane immediately.

ONE WHEEL RETRACTED (HARD GROUND).

Ordinarily a wheels-up landing is preferable to a landing with only one wheel extended. However, if one wheel is extended and cannot be retracted, proceed as follows:

1. Make normal flaps-down approach, with wing low on the extended-gear side.

2. Touch down on main wheel and tail wheel simultaneously. Use ailerons to hold up wing with retracted gear.

3. Shut down engine.

4. Maintain controlled ground roll by use of steerable tail wheel and brake.

5. When wing tip strikes the ground, apply maximum brake pressure possible without raising the tail.

Note

If the landing area permits, a decrease in ground speed can be obtained before the wing tip strikes the ground, by turning in the direction of the retracted gear.

FLAT TIRE.

If a tire is flat at the time of landing or a blowout occurs during the ground roll, proceed as follows:

1. Hold stick full back to keep tail down and apply full aileron opposite the flat tire.

2. Apply brake hard to wheel opposite the flat tire and use steerable tail wheel to try to maintain a controlled landing roll.

3. Shut down engine.

EMERGENCY PANEL RELEASE TYPICAL FOR BOTH SIDES—EACH COCKPIT

Figure 3-5. Emergency Escape on the Ground

EMERGENCY ENTRANCE.

The canopy lever on the exterior left side of each canopy is used for entrance to either cockpit in an emergency.

EMERGENCY ESCAPE ON THE GROUND.

If the canopy cannot be opened, emergency escape can be accomplished through a removable canopy panel (figure 3-5) on each side of both cockpits.

DITCHING.

The airplane should be ditched only as a last resort. Since all emergency equipment is carried by the pilots, there is no advantage in riding the airplane down. However, if for some reason bail-out is impossible and ditching is unavoidable, proceed as follows:

Be sure to ditch while fuel is still available.

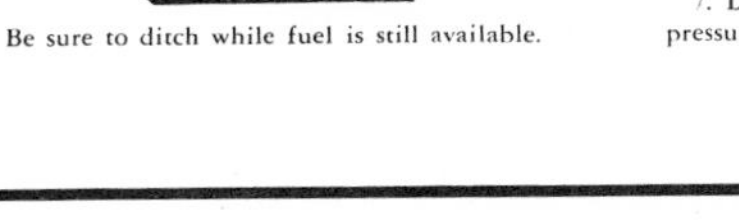

1. Follow radio distress procedure.

2. Turn battery switch OFF.

3. See that no personal equipment will foul when you leave the airplane.

4. Unbuckle parachute and release the life raft from the parachute harness. Tighten and lock safety belt and shoulder harness, as there is a violent deceleration of the airplane upon final impact.

CAUTION

Before locking shoulder harness, turn off all switches not readily accessible with the harness locked.

5. Check landing gear handle UP.

6. Canopy full open and locked.

7. Lower wing flaps 20 degrees if sufficient hydraulic pressure is available.

8. Make normal approach with power if possible and flare out to a normal landing attitude. Touch down, approaching stalling speed with tail low. Unless the wind is high or the sea is rough, plan the approach heading parallel to any uniform swell pattern and try to touch down along a wave crest or just after a crest has passed. If the wind is as high as 40 mph or the surface is irregular, the best procedure is to approach into the wind and touch down on the falling side of the wave.

9. Just before impact, turn ignition switch OFF.

10. The back cushion of both cockpit seats is filled with kapok and may be used as a life preserver.

11. When leaving airplane, be sure to carry life raft with you.

BAIL-OUT.

In the event the decision has been made to abandon the airplane in flight, the following steps should be taken:

1. Reduce airplane speed as much as possible; trim it slightly nose-down and head for an uninhabited area.

2. Warn the other pilot to bail out and receive his acknowledgment.

3. See that no personal equipment will foul when you bail out.

4. Raise seat to top position.

5. Canopy full open and locked.

Note

If the canopy cannot be opened, raise the red release handle at the bottom center of either panel, breaking the safety wire, and push the panel clear of the airplane.

6. From either cockpit, dive toward trailing edge of wing. (See figure 3-6.)

FUEL SYSTEM EMERGENCY OPERATION.

If the engine-driven fuel pump fails, fuel can be supplied to the engine by operating the hand fuel pump on the left side of each cockpit.

ELECTRICAL POWER SYSTEM EMERGENCY OPERATION.

If the ammeter shows zero current during flight, it may indicate failure of the generator system. In such case, the battery will supply the electrical load for a short time only. Turn the generator switch OFF and conserve the battery by using electrical equipment sparingly. If a complete electrical failure should occur or if it becomes necessary to turn off both the generator and battery switches, landing should be made as soon as possible. See figure 1-17 for electrically operated equipment.

HYDRAULIC POWER SYSTEM EMERGENCY OPERATION.

Hydraulic hand-pump can be used to operate the landing gear or flaps should the engine-driven pump fail. It is not necessary to move the power control lever when the hand-pump is used, since a check valve in the system separates the hand-pump from the power control valve. To operate landing gear or flaps by means of the hand-pump:

1. Place the landing gear handle or wing flap handle in the desired position.

2. Raise the hand-pump handle to the extended position, turn handle clockwise until it locks, and operate the pump.

The wing flaps cannot be operated in case of complete hydraulic failure. The landing gear, however, can be lowered by gravity when hydraulic pressure is unavailable.

LANDING GEAR SYSTEM EMERGENCY OPERATION.

LANDING GEAR EMERGENCY LOWERING.

The procedure for lowering the landing gear in case of complete hydraulic failure is given in figure 3-7.

LANDING GEAR EMERGENCY DOWNLOCK.

Should the landing gear fail to automatically lock in the down position, move the front cockpit landing gear handle down to the extreme end of the sector (EMERGENCY position). This manually forces the downlock pins in place to lock the gear down. However, the handle must never be positioned to EMERGENCY *before* the gear is completely down; if it is, while the handle is at

Figure 3-6. Bail-out

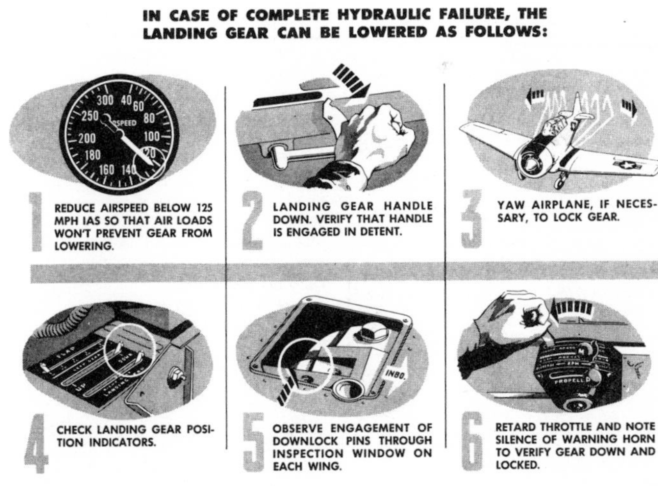

Figure 3-7. Landing Gear Emergency Lowering

EMERGENCY, the downlock pins may prevent the gear from extending fully.

Note

The landing gear downlock pins can be visually checked for locked position through a window in the wing above the landing gear strut.

HAND-CRANKING ENGINE.

If electrical power is not available, the starter can be energized manually by a handcrank as follows:

1. Move the brush spring release handle on the back of the starter to OFF (clockwise). The handle can be reached through an access door on the upper left side of the engine compartment cowling.

2. Insert handcrank into opening provided forward of the access door and rotate at approximately 80 rpm.

3. When this speed has been attained, remove handcrank and pull manual engaging ring located above crank opening.

4. After engine starts, release engaging ring, return brush-spring release handle to ON and safety with wire; then stow crank in baggage compartment.

DESCRIPTION AND OPERATION OF

AUXILIARY EQUIPMENT

SECTION IV

HEATING SYSTEM.

Ram air from a duct opening on the top front of the engine is heated in a shroud around the exhaust manifold and is then introduced into the front cockpit. The cockpit hot-air temperature control valve (4, figure 1-11) is located inboard of the right rudder pedal. A butterfly valve in the outlet can be rotated by the pilot's foot to regulate the volume of hot air entering the cockpit.

VENTILATING SYSTEM.

Cold air for ventilating is obtained from an opening in the leading edge of the left wing center section and is discharged in the front cockpit from a cold-air temperature control valve (5, figure 1-11), located inboard of the left rudder pedal. The outlet, which incorporates a butterfly valve, can be adjusted by the pilot's foot to control the volume of air entering the cockpits. A ventilator on the left side of the rear cockpit can be manually opened by a handle (17, figure 1-9) to provide fresh air for the rear cockpit. Additional ventilation may be obtained by opening the sliding sections of the canopy to any one of the intermediate positions.

PITOT HEATER.

A heater in the pitot head is controlled by the pitot heater switch (figure 1-6), located on the instrument subpanel in the front cockpit only.

CAUTION

To prevent burning out heater elements, the pitot heater switch should be OFF when the airplane is on the ground.

COMMUNICATIONS AND ASSOCIATED ELECTRONIC EQUIPMENT.

TABLE OF COMMUNICATIONS AND ASSOCIATED ELECTRONIC EQUIPMENT.

TYPE	DESIGNATION	USE	HORIZONTAL RANGE	LOCATION OF CONTROLS
VHF command	AN/ARC-3	Two-way communication	30 miles at 1000 feet, 135 miles at 10,000 feet	Figures 1-5 and 1-10
Radio compass	AN/ARN-7	Reception of voice and code communication, position finding, homing	50 to 100 miles for range signals, 100 to 250 miles for broadcast signals	Figure 4-1
Radio range receiver	BC-453	Radio range reception	50 to 70 miles	Figure 1-5
Interphone	AN/AIC-2	Intercockpit communication		Figures 1-5 and 1-10
Marker beacon	RC-193A	Reception of location marker signals (fan marker)		Figures 1-3 and 1-8

COMMUNICATIONS MASTER CONTROLS.

COMMUNICATIONS CONTROL JACK BOX. A jack box for control of the communications equipment, located on the right side of each cockpit, incorporates a master volume control knob (6, figure 1-5; 1, figure 1-10) and a master selector switch (7, figure 1-5; 13, figure 1-10). Moving the selector switch to COMP, VHF, RANGE, or INTER selects the radio compass, command set, radio range receiver, and interphone, respectively. The selector switch is spring-loaded from CALL to INTER. The CALL position is used to interrupt any radio reception in the airplane to enable immediate interphone communication without transmitting the conversation. The master volume control knob, marked "INCREASE OUTPUT," increases reception volume when rotated clockwise.

RADIO RANGE FILTER SWITCH. The radio range filter switch (8, figure 1-5; 2, figure 1-10) is mounted on a panel in each cockpit aft of the communications control jack box. Placing the selector in the RANGE position subdues voice reception to bring out range reception. Moving the selector to the VOICE position causes radio range signals to be subdued to bring out voice reception. In the BOTH position, voice and range receptions are received in equal volume.

VHF COMMAND RADIO CONTROL AND INDICATOR.

In addition to the conventional controls, the vhf command radio also incorporates control transfer switches and control indicator lights.

VHF CONTROL TRANSFER SWITCH. A control transfer switch (11, figure 1-5; 5, figure 1-10), mounted on the vhf control panel in each cockpit, is provided to enable either pilot to control channel selection of the vhf command radio. This switch has no effect on reception of radio signals.

VHF CONTROL INDICATOR LIGHT. A control indicator light (13, figure 1-5; 4, figure 1-10) is located on the vhf control panel in each cockpit. The light illuminates in the cockpit from which the command set can be controlled as determined by the vhf control transfer switch.

OPERATION OF VHF COMMAND RADIO.

1. Position vhf control transfer switch so that the vhf control indicator light illuminates.

2. Depress desired channel selector button.

3. Allow 30 to 40 seconds for set to warm up. Near the end of warm-up period, an audio tone will be heard in the headset. When the tone stops, the set is ready for operation and may be tuned.

4. Adjust vhf audio control knob for desired output. Rotate control clockwise to increase volume.

5. Depress the press-to-talk button on the microphone to transmit; release the button to receive. Reception will be cut off at both crew stations whenever either microphone button is depressed.

Note

Do not turn command radio off immediately after depressing a channel selector button. If the automatic selector has not had sufficient time to complete its change cycle, the set will be inoperative when it is again turned on. Should this occur, turn the set on by pressing any channel selector button and run through the complete number of selections. Then depress the desired selector button, and the set will resume normal operation.

OPERATION OF RADIO COMPASS.

1. Position CW selector switch at bottom of radio compass control panel at VOICE. For reception of continuous wave transmission, place CW selector switch to CW position.

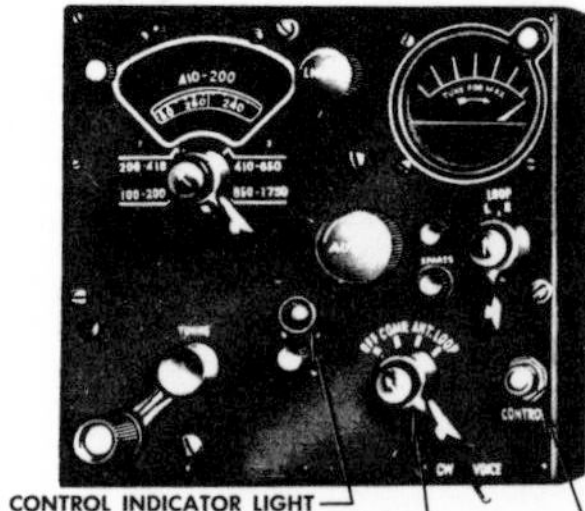

Figure 4-1. Radio Compass Control Panel

2. With master selector switch on the control jack box at COMP, turn radio compass power switch on radio compass control panel to ANT.

3. Depress control button on radio compass control panel to obtain control of set. When control is complete, the indicator on the tuning meter fluctuates and the green control indicator light illuminates.

4. Rotate frequency band selector on radio compass control panel to desired frequency band.

5. Rotate tuning crank to tune in desired frequency as indicated by maximum deflection of the indicator on the tuning meter. Proper station is identified by published call sign.

6. Place radio compass power switch at COMP to actuate indicator hand on radio compass.

7. When using the radio compass for aural-null procedures, the set should be tuned for maximum readability rather than maximum deflection of the tuning meter. For maximum reception or aural-null orientation and homing, the loop antenna can be rotated by using the loop adjustment switch on the radio compass control panel. Pushing the switch in against a spring load and moving it to L or R causes the loop antenna to revolve rapidly for large adjustments. In the normal position to which the switch is spring-loaded, its movement causes the loop to revolve slowly for fine adjustments. The radio compass power switch should be at LOOP for adjustment of the loop antenna.

RADIO RANGE RECEIVER CONTROL.

The range receiver can be tuned from the front cockpit only. In addition to the conventional controls, the range receiver also includes a range-volume switch.

RANGE-VOLUME SWITCH. A range-volume switch (10, figure 1-5), located in the front cockpit, has two positions—FORWARD COCKPIT and AFT COCKPIT. The switch enables the radio range receiver volume to be individually controlled from the selected cockpit.

OPERATION OF RADIO RANGE RECEIVER.

1. Place master selector switch on control jack box to RANGE.

2. Move range receiver power switch on range receiver control box from OFF to MCW for voice or radio range reception.

3. Place range receiver A-B switch on range receiver control box at A.

4. Rotate tuning crank on range receiver control box to tune set to desired frequency as indicated by revolving dial.

5. Rotate master volume control knob on control jack box fully clockwise for maximum output.

6. Set range-volume switch (in front cockpit) at FORWARD COCKPIT CONTROL and AFT COCKPIT, respectively, so that radio range volume can be adjusted as desired by each pilot.

7. Adjust volume of range reception with volume control, marked INCREASE OUTPUT. The volume control increases volume as it is rotated clockwise.

OPERATION OF INTERPHONE.

1. Place master selector switch on control jack box at INTER.

2. Use microphone as in normal radio transmission.

3. To receive vhf command set signals while using interphone, place vhf audio switch on vhf control panel at ON. This allows reception of selected frequency channel without transmitting interphone conversation.

OPERATION OF MARKER BEACON.

The marker beacon receiver operates automatically when the battery-disconnect switch is turned ON.

LIGHTING EQUIPMENT.

EXTERIOR LIGHT CONTROLS.

All exterior lights (landing, position, passing, and recognition) are controlled from the front cockpit only. See figure 4-2 for location of all exterior lights.

Do not leave landing, passing, or recognition lights on for more than 10 seconds when airplane is on the ground, as excess heat may seriously damage the lights.

LANDING LIGHT SWITCHES. Landing lights, installed in the leading edge of each outer wing panel, are individually turned ON and OFF by switches (figure 1-6) located on the instrument subpanel in the front cockpit.

POSITION LIGHT SWITCHES. Position lights, located on the wing tips and tail, are controlled by switches (figure 1-6) located on the instrument subpanel in the front cockpit. Individual switches for the wing and tail have BRIGHT, DIM, and OFF positions. The left wing lights are red, the right wing lights are green, and the taillights are white.

Figure 4-2. Exterior Lights

PASSING LIGHT SWITCH. A passing light, installed in the leading edge of the left wing beside the landing light, is turned ON and OFF by a switch (figure 1-6) located on the instrument subpanel in the front cockpit.

RECOGNITION LIGHT SWITCHES. Three recognition lights (red, green, and amber) are installed on the lower side of the fuselage just aft of the rear cockpit. A white recognition light is located aft of the rear cockpit on the top of the fuselage. The lights are turned on and off by individual switches (figure 1-6), located on the panel adjacent to the instrument subpanel in the front cockpit. Each individual switch can be placed in the KEY, STEADY, or OFF position. With any switch in the KEY position, the push-button on the top of the switch panel can be used to flash the related light as desired. The recognition lights are disconnected on most airplanes.

INTERIOR LIGHT CONTROLS.

INSTRUMENT PANEL LIGHT RHEOSTAT. The instrument panels are illuminated by fluorescent lights, one on each side of each cockpit. The lights are controlled by individual rheostats (figure 1-6; 9 and 11, figure 1-10), located on the instrument subpanel in the front cockpit and on the electrical control panel in the rear cockpit, respectively.

COCKPIT LIGHT CONTROL KNOB. A cockpit light is mounted on the left side of each cockpit. The light beam can be adjusted from a small spotlight to a floodlight beam. Light brilliancy is controlled by a knob (3, figures 1-4 and 1-9) on the side of the lamp housing. A push-button switch on the back of the lamp housing provides a means of instantaneous control of the light so that it may be used for signaling. The head of the lamp housing, which contains a red lens, can be removed to obtain a white light. The lamp can be removed from its bracket and held in any desired position.

FUEL QUANTITY GAGE LIGHT SWITCH. Lights above each fuel quantity gage can be turned ON or OFF from either cockpit. The fuel quantity gage light switch (figure 1-6) in the front cockpit is located on the instrument subpanel; the switch (10, figure 1-10) in the rear cockpit is on the electrical control panel.

COMPASS LIGHT RHEOSTAT. Illumination of each magnetic compass is controlled by a rheostat (figure 1-6; 8, figure 1-10) in each cockpit. The rheostat in the front cockpit is located on the instrument subpanel; in the rear cockpit, the rheostat is on the electrical control panel.

RADIO COMPASS CONTROL PANEL LIGHT RHEOSTAT. A rheostat (figure 4-1), labeled "LIGHTS," is located at the top of the radio compass control panel in each cockpit. The rheostat turns on and regulates the brilliance of the self-contained radio compass control panel lights. The rheostat moves clockwise from its off position, which is marked by a white radial line.

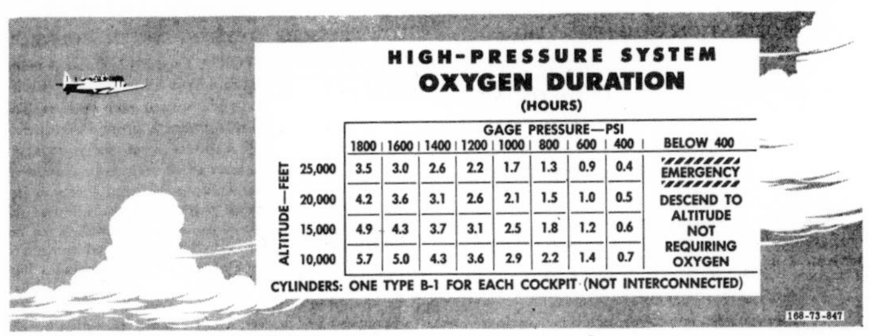

ALTITUDE—FEET	GAGE PRESSURE—PSI 1800	1600	1400	1200	1000	800	600	400	BELOW 400
25,000	3.5	3.0	2.6	2.2	1.7	1.3	0.9	0.4	EMERGENCY
20,000	4.2	3.6	3.1	2.6	2.1	1.5	1.0	0.5	DESCEND TO ALTITUDE NOT REQUIRING OXYGEN
15,000	4.9	4.3	3.7	3.1	2.5	1.8	1.2	0.6	
10,000	5.7	5.0	4.3	3.6	2.9	2.2	1.4	0.7	

Figure 4-3. Oxygen Duration (High-pressure System)

OXYGEN SYSTEM.

The airplanes were originally delivered with either a high-pressure or a low-pressure oxygen system. The oxygen system on most airplanes has since been rendered inoperative.

HIGH-PRESSURE OXYGEN SYSTEM.

An individual, high-pressure oxygen system is provided for each cockpit. A separate Type B-1 oxygen cylinder supplies each system. The oxygen cylinders, installed behind the baggage compartment, must be removed from the airplane to be serviced. An oxygen regulator, incorporating a flow indicator and pressure gage, is installed in each cockpit. The approximate duration of the oxygen supply in man-hours for each separate system is given in figure 4-3.

HIGH-PRESSURE OXYGEN SYSTEM CONTROL.

OXYGEN REGULATOR. A Type A-8 oxygen regulator (figure 4-4) is located below the instrument panel on the right side of each cockpit. The regulator supplies a continuous flow of oxygen, the concentration of which is determined by the setting of an incorporated control knob. The control knob should be set so that the flow indicator reading corresponds to the altitude at which the airplane is flying.

HIGH-PRESSURE OXYGEN SYSTEM INDICATORS.

OXYGEN PRESSURE GAGE. A pressure gage (figure 4-4), located on the lower half of the regulator dial, registers the pressure in the oxygen cylinder for the respective cockpit.

OXYGEN FLOW INDICATOR. A flow indicator (figure 4-4) is located on the upper half of the regulator dial. The indicator is set by the regulator control knob to a reading that corresponds to the airplane altitude. This setting will provide oxygen in sufficient quantity for the particular altitude.

HIGH-PRESSURE OXYGEN SYSTEM OPERATION.

PREFLIGHT CHECK. Prior to each flight requiring use of oxygen, check system as follows:

1. Check oxygen pressure gage for normal pressure of 1800 psi (500 psi minimum).
2. Check oxygen mask for fit and absence of leakage.
3. Attach mask tube to regulator outlet and check connection for security.
4. Open regulator control knob until the flow indicator registers 15,000 feet. Restrict the mask outlet valves by hand and note that rebreather bag inflates to verify that oxygen is being supplied.
5. Remove mask and close regulator control knob.

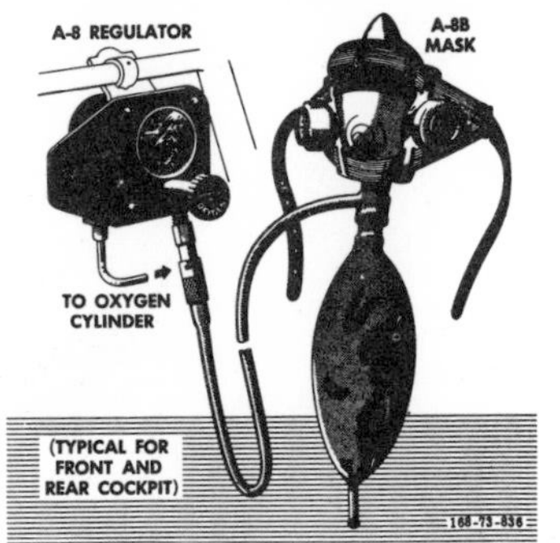

Figure 4-4. High-pressure Oxygen System—Regulator and Mask

NORMAL OPERATION. During flight, check oxygen system as follows:

1. Open regulator control knob until reading on flow indicator corresponds with altitude at which the airplane is flying.
2. Check connection of mask tube to regulator outlet.
3. Check cylinder pressure frequently for oxygen system pressure, and determine duration.
4. Check flow indicator frequently, especially during changes in altitude, to verify that reading corresponds with airplane altitude.

Note

To ensure an adequate supply of oxygen during ascent or periods of unusual activity, the flow indicator reading should be set about 5000 feet higher than airplane altitude.

LOW-PRESSURE OXYGEN SYSTEM.

The low-pressure oxygen system is supplied by four Type D-2 oxygen cylinders installed behind the baggage compartment. A filler valve, also located in the baggage compartment, is provided to service the cylinders. A diluter-demand oxygen regulator, flow indicator, and pressure gage are installed in each cockpit. The approximate oxygen duration for each pilot is given in figure 4-5.

LOW-PRESSURE OXYGEN SYSTEM CONTROL.

OXYGEN REGULATOR. A Type A-12 diluter-demand oxygen regulator (figure 4-6) is located below the instrument panel on the right side of each cockpit. The regulator automatically supplies a proper mixture of air and oxygen at all altitudes when set at NORMAL OXYGEN. The diluter lever of the regulator should always be set at NORMAL OXYGEN position except under emergency conditions; if it is not, the duration of the oxygen system will be considerably reduced. With the diluter lever at 100% OXYGEN, undiluted oxygen is supplied at any altitude whenever the user inhales. The emergency valve of the regulator is safety-wired closed and should be opened only if the regulator becomes inoperative. The valve, when opened (by turning the knob counterclockwise), directs a steady stream of oxygen into the mask.

LOW-PRESSURE OXYGEN SYSTEM INDICATORS.

OXYGEN PRESSURE GAGE. A pressure gage (figure 4-6), located adjacent to the regulator in each cockpit, registers oxygen cylinder pressure.

OXYGEN FLOW INDICATOR. A flow indicator (figure 4-6) is located adjacent to the regulator and pressure gage in each cockpit. The flow indicator shows that oxygen is flowing through the regulator, but not how much oxygen is flowing. The "eye" of the indicator blinks with each breath of the user. When the emergency valve is opened, the indicator does not blink.

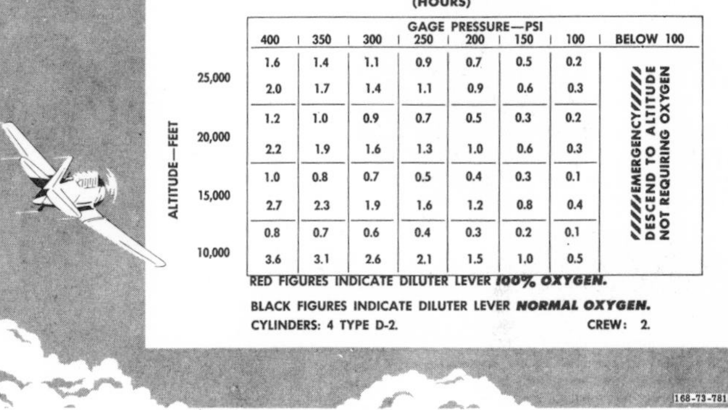

ALTITUDE—FEET	GAGE PRESSURE—PSI 400	350	300	250	200	150	100	BELOW 100
25,000	1.6	1.4	1.1	0.9	0.7	0.5	0.2	EMERGENCY DESCEND TO ALTITUDE NOT REQUIRING OXYGEN
	2.0	1.7	1.4	1.1	0.9	0.6	0.3	
20,000	1.2	1.0	0.9	0.7	0.5	0.3	0.2	
	2.2	1.9	1.6	1.3	1.0	0.6	0.3	
15,000	1.0	0.8	0.7	0.5	0.4	0.3	0.1	
	2.7	2.3	1.9	1.6	1.2	0.8	0.4	
10,000	0.8	0.7	0.6	0.4	0.3	0.2	0.1	
	3.6	3.1	2.6	2.1	1.5	1.0	0.5	

Figure 4-5. Oxygen Duration (Low-pressure System)

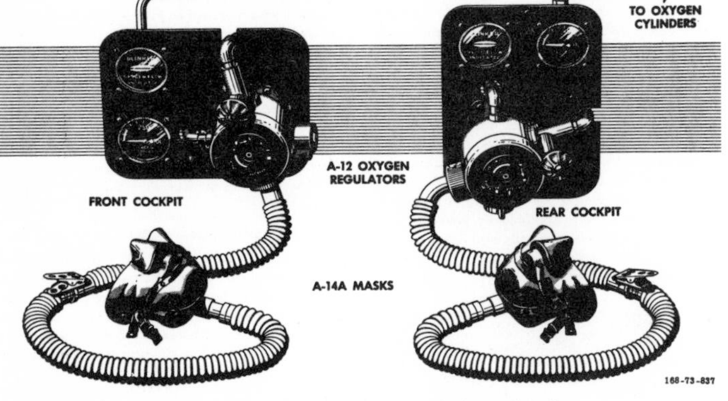

Figure 4-6. Low-pressure Oxygen System—Regulator and Mask

LOW-PRESSURE OXYGEN SYSTEM OPERATION.

PREFLIGHT CHECK. Prior to each flight requiring use of oxygen, check system as follows:

1. Check oxygen pressure gage for indication between 400 and 450 psi.
2. Check oxygen mask for fit and absence of leakage.
3. Connect mask tube to regulator outlet. Check connection for tightness. Attach tube clip to parachute harness, high enough to permit free movement of head without pinching or pulling hose.
4. Breathe normally on oxygen regulator several times with diluter lever at NORMAL OXYGEN and then at 100% OXYGEN to check flow from oxygen regulator and operation of flow indicator.
5. Check oxygen regulator to see that emergency valve is safety-wired closed and the diluter lever is in NORMAL OXYGEN position.

NORMAL OPERATION. During flight, check oxygen system as follows:

1. Diluter lever at NORMAL OXYGEN position.
2. Check connection of mask tube to regulator tube.
3. Check flow indicator frequently for flow of oxygen.
4. Check pressure gage frequently for oxygen system pressure, and determine duration.

EMERGENCY OPERATION. Should drowsiness indicate the onset of anoxia, or if smoke or fuel fumes should enter the cockpit, set the diluter lever of the oxygen regulator to 100% OXYGEN. If the oxygen regulator should become inoperative, open the emergency valve by turning the red emergency knob counterclockwise.

After emergency is over, set diluter lever of oxygen regulator to NORMAL OXYGEN, and check to ascertain that emergency valve is closed.

ARMAMENT EQUIPMENT.

All airplanes have provisions for armament, which includes bombing equipment, machine guns, gun sight, and camera. The armament equipment derives its electrical power from the 28-volt direct-current system. Although provisions are made for armament equipment in all airplanes, only a few are utilized for gunnery and bombing practice.

BOMBING EQUIPMENT.

Bombing equipment includes provisions for a flush-type bomb rack on the lower surface of each outer wing panel. The bomb rack will carry five 30-pound or five 20-pound bombs. Auxiliary bomb shackles can be added to these racks for carrying two 100-pound bombs under each wing. The bomb release button, selector switch, safety switch, and nose fuse switch are incorporated in all airplanes; however, the bomb-arming handle, release handle, and emergency salvo handle have been removed.

GUNNERY EQUIPMENT.

Gunnery equipment consists of complete provisions for installation and operation of two fixed machine guns (one on the fuselage and one on the wing). A gun camera is provided for recording marksmanship proficiency when firing on a target. Provisions have been made in the rear cockpit to install, operate, and stow a flexible machine gun.

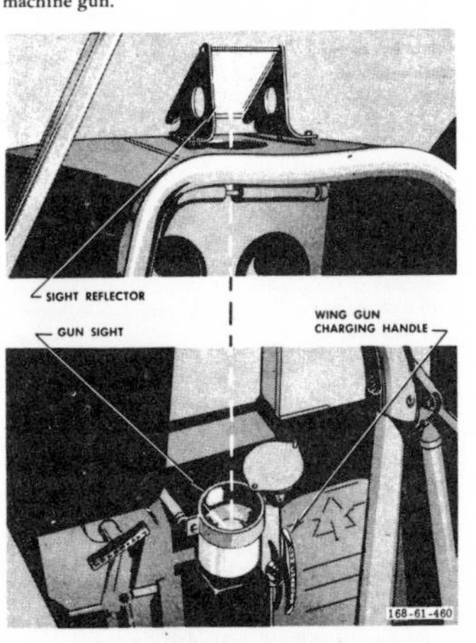

Figure 4-7. Gun Sight (Early Airplanes) and Wing Gun Charger

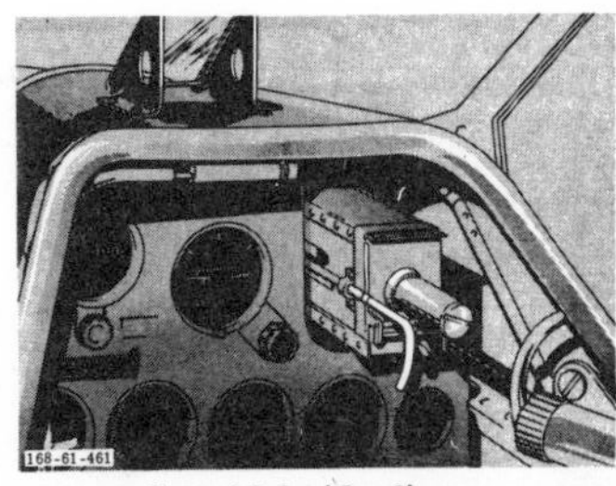

Figure 4-8. Cowl Gun Charger

GUNS.

The fixed Type M-2 .30-caliber fuselage machine gun (figure 4-8), mounted in the top of the engine cowl, is synchronized to fire through the propeller arc and is supplied with 200 rounds of ammunition. The other fixed Type M-2 .30-caliber machine gun is mounted in the right outer wing panel and is supplied with 250 rounds of ammunition. The rear cockpit incorporates provisions for installation of a Type M-2 .30-caliber flexible machine gun for azimuth and elevation firing. The flexible gun is supplied with 500 rounds of ammunition. There are no automatic provisions incorporated to prevent inadvertent damage to the airplane from firing the flexible gun.

GUN CONTROLS.

GUN SAFETY SWITCH. Electrical power to operate the fixed guns is controlled by a gun safety switch (figure 1-6), located on the instrument subpanel in the front cockpit. The switch has two positions, FIRE and SAFE.

GUN SELECTOR SWITCHES. Two selector switches (figure 1-6), located on the front cockpit instrument subpanel, are provided for the fixed guns. Electrical power to the guns is interrupted when the switches are OFF. Either or both fixed guns may be selected for firing by placing the respective switches to ON.

GUN TRIGGER. A gun trigger (20, figure 1-5), located on the control stick grip, is provided to fire the fixed guns.

GUN CHARGING HANDLES. The wing gun charging handle (figure 4-7) is located in the front cockpit below the instrument panel. The cowl gun charging handle (figure 4-8) is located near the upper right corner of the instrument panel in the front cockpit. Pulling the charging handle of either gun back to the limit of travel will charge the respective gun or eject a defective cartridge.

GUN SIGHT.

The N-3B gun sight is a fixed-reticle sight. Early airplanes incorporate the sight reflector above the center of the front instrument panel shroud and the main gun sight directly below the front instrument panel. (See figure 4-7.) Later airplanes incorporate the sight and sight reflector in the center of the instrument panel shroud in the front cockpit. (See figure 4-9.) The intensity of the sight reticle illumination may be adjusted from full brilliance to OFF, by means of the gun sight rheostat (figure 1-6) on the instrument subpanel in the front cockpit. The sight reflector is installed for a gun sighting position, in which the line of sight is parallel to the flight path of the airplane. The principle of operation is the apparent projection of the reticle image in space, which is similar to having the reticle image superimposed on the target. The old-style ring-and-bead sight required the pilot to keep his eye carefully fixed in relation to the ring and bead; however, on the N-3B sight reflector, slight movement of the pilot's head does not cause misalignment of the sight reticle image and the target.

GUN CAMERA.

Early airplanes incorporate a W-7B gun camera installed in the leading edge of the left wing. Later airplanes incorporate an N-2 GSAP camera (figure 4-9) installed adjacent to the gun sight in the front cockpit. The camera is electrically driven when the trigger on the control stick grip is depressed and the camera switch

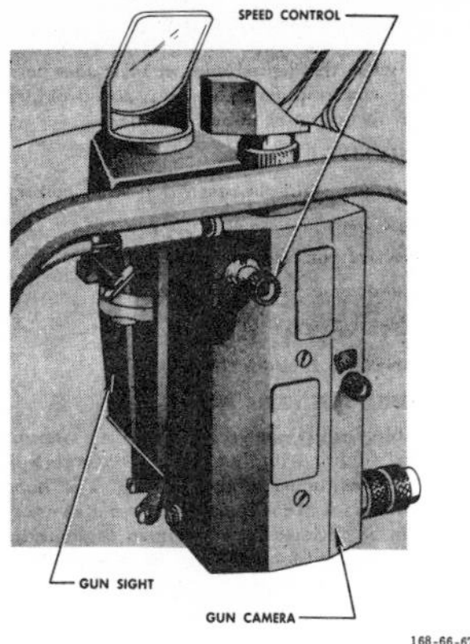

Figure 4-9. Gun Sight and Camera (Late Airplanes)

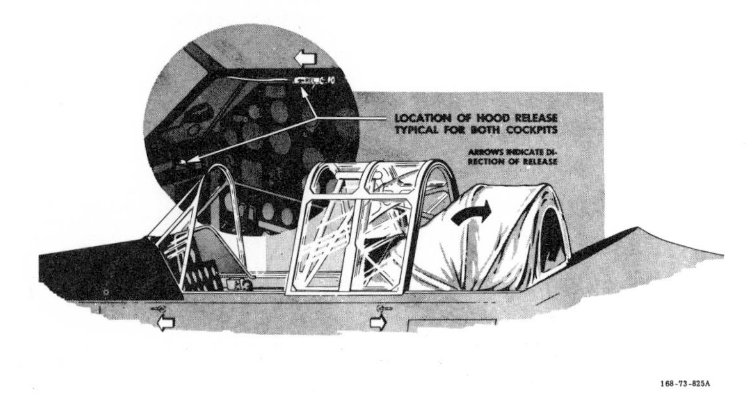

Figure 4-10. Instrument Flying Hood and Controls

(figure 1-6), located on the instrument subpanel, is at the FIRE position. A speed control is provided on the camera to select the desired number of frames per second. A film consumption indicator is also provided to register the feet of unused film remaining.

FIRING FIXED GUNS.

1. Adjust gun sight rheostat for desired brilliancy.
2. Charge guns.
3. Respective gun selector switch ON.
4. Gun and camera safety switches FIRE.
5. Depress trigger.

MISCELLANEOUS EQUIPMENT.

INSTRUMENT FLYING HOOD.

Both cockpits incorporate provisions for an instrument flying hood (figure 4-10), but only the rear cockpit is enclosed for instrument flight training. The hood is stowed at the back of the cockpit when not in use. The cockpit can be enclosed for instrument flight training by pulling the hood forward and engaging it with the latch at the top of the instrument panel shroud. The hood is provided with an elastic bungee to facilitate release.

INSTRUMENT FLYING HOOD CONTROLS. Each cockpit is provided with an instrument flying hood release handle and latch lever. The release handle (8, figure 1-4; 7, figure 1-9), located at the forward left side of the cockpit, can be actuated for normal release of the hood or, in an emergency, for release of the hood in the other cockpit. A latch lever (figure 4-10), incorporated in the engaging latch (below the top of the instrument panel shroud), can also be used as a normal release for the instrument flying hood. The latch lever cannot release the hood in the adjoining cockpit.

Be sure that there is adequate head clearance before releasing instrument flying hood.

MAP, DATA, AND FLIGHT REPORT CASES.

A map and data case is provided on the right side of the front cockpit, on the left side of the rear cockpit, and in the baggage compartment. A flight report case is installed on the right side of the front cockpit.

RELIEF TUBE.

A relief tube is attached to a bracket at the bottom of each seat.

CHECK LISTS.

A Pilot's Training and Transition Check List is provided in each cockpit in a location that is convenient and has adequate clearance with all controls to prevent interference.

OPERATING LIMITATIONS.

Some of the recommended operating conditions of the airplane or its component systems can be exceeded in the air or on the ground. The gages that indicate these operating ranges are marked in red to show the maximum safe limit. Instrument markings showing the various operating limits are illustrated in figure 5-1. In some cases, the markings represent limitations that are self-explanatory and therefore are not discussed in the text. Operating restrictions or limitations which do not appear as maximum limits on the cockpit instruments are completely discussed in the following paragraphs.

MINIMUM CREW REQUIREMENTS.

Solo flight is permissible in this airplane; however, on solo flights the airplane must be flown from the front cockpit. Solo flight from the rear cockpit is prohibited because of insufficient controls and visibility restrictions.

ENGINE LIMITATIONS.

All normal engine limitations are shown in figure 5-1. The maximum allowable engine overspeed is 2800 rpm for 30 seconds.

Whenever engine speed exceeds the operating limits, the airplane should be landed immediately at the nearest base. The reason for the overspeed (if known), the maximum rpm, and duration will be entered in Form 1 and reported to the maintenance officer. Overspeed between 2800 and 2900 rpm will necessitate an inspection of he engine before further flight. If the rpm exceeded 2900, the engine will be removed for overhaul.

PROPELLER LIMITATIONS.

Because of undesirable harmonic vibration frequencies, prolonged ground operation betwen 1450 and 1800 rpm is prohibited. This restriction does not apply during flight, because airflow through the propeller is directly from the front and therefore does not set up any harmonic vibrations.

AIRSPEED LIMITATIONS.

The red line on the airspeed indicator marks the limit dive speed at any altitude. The limit dive speed for the airplane with external loads is the same as for the clean airplane. However, the airplane should not be dived to airspeeds in excess of those where light to moderate airplane or surface control buffet is experienced. The yellow line indicates the maximum airspeed at which the flaps may be lowered to the full down position. The maximum airspeed for landing gear down is not marked on the airspeed indicator but is given below the indicator on figure 5-1. Lowering either the flaps or gear at speeds in excess of the flaps-down or gear-down limit airspeeds may cause structural damage to the airplane. Because of the danger of accidental stalls, the minimum permissible indicated airspeed during sideslips is 90 mph.

PROHIBITED MANEUVERS.

Outside loops, inverted spins, snap rolls in excess of 130 mph, and slow rolls in excess of 190 mph are prohibited. Inverted flight must be limited to 10 seconds, as there is no means of ensuring a continuous flow of fuel or oil in this attitude. Also, prolonged inverted flight can cause an accumulation of hydrogen gas in the battery at sufficient pressure to continuously hold the vents closed until the battery eventually explodes. Since altitude is lost rapidly during a sideslip, this maneuver should not be attempted below 200 feet.

All acrobatic maneuvers performed during training flights should be completed at least 5000 feet above the ground.

ACCELERATION LIMITS.

The airplane is limited to a maximum positive G-load of 5.67 and a maximum negative G-load of –2.33. These limits apply only when the clean airplane gross weight does not exceed 5300 pounds (design gross weight). When airplane gross weight is greater than 5300 pounds, the maximum allowable G-load is less than the maximum limit marked on the accelerometer. Remember that when you pull the maximum G-load (5.67 G), the wings of your airplane must support 5.67 times their normal load. This means that during a maximum G pull-out the wings of the airplane (at design gross weight) are supporting 5.67 times 5300 pounds, or a total of approximately 30,000 pounds (maximum that the wings can safely support). Therefore, when your airplane weighs more than 5300 pounds, the maximum G-load that you can safely apply can be determined by dividing 30,000 by the new gross weight. When external loads are carried, the maximum allowable G-load is limited to 4.3 G. The maximum G-loads we have been talking about apply only to straight pull-outs. Rolling pull-outs are a different story however, since they impose considerably more stress upon the airplane. The maximum allowable G-load in a rolling pull-out is limited to two-thirds the maximum G-load for a straight pull-out.

AIRPLANE STRENGTH — G-LOAD.

The strength diagram (figure 5-2) shows the strength limitations of the airplane. Various G-loads are shown vertically along the left side of the chart, and various indicated airspeeds are shown horizontally across the center of the chart. The horizontal red lines at the top and bottom of the chart represent the maximum positive and maximum negative allowable G-loads. The vertical red line indicates the limit dive speed of the airplane. The curved lines show the G-load at which the airplane will stall at various airspeeds. The upper curved line shows, for example, that at 100 mph the airplane will stall in a 2 G turn, while at 150 mph the airplane will not stall until more than 4 G is applied. The upper and lower limits at the right side of the chart illustrate that the maximum positive and negative limit load factors (+5.67G and –2.33 G) can be safely applied up to the limit dive speed of the airplane.

CENTER-OF-GRAVITY LIMITATIONS.

Any configuration of external load that the airplane is designed to carry may be installed without exceeding the CG limits. There is only one possible loading condition that could cause the airplane CG to exceed its limitation. This could occur when fuel supply is low on a solo flight with no baggage. The result would be a slightly nose-heavy condition. Therefore, when this situation is encountered, additional care must be exercised during the flare-out (to prevent a two-point touchdown with the possibility of striking the propeller) and immediately after the touchdown (to prevent nosing over). However, this nose-heavy condition can be prevented by carrying a load of approximately 100 pounds in the baggage compartment to keep the CG within limits.

WEIGHT LIMITATIONS.

The maximum allowable gross weight of the airplane cannot be exceeded. However, the baggage compartment should not be loaded in excess of its maximum capacity of 100 pounds.

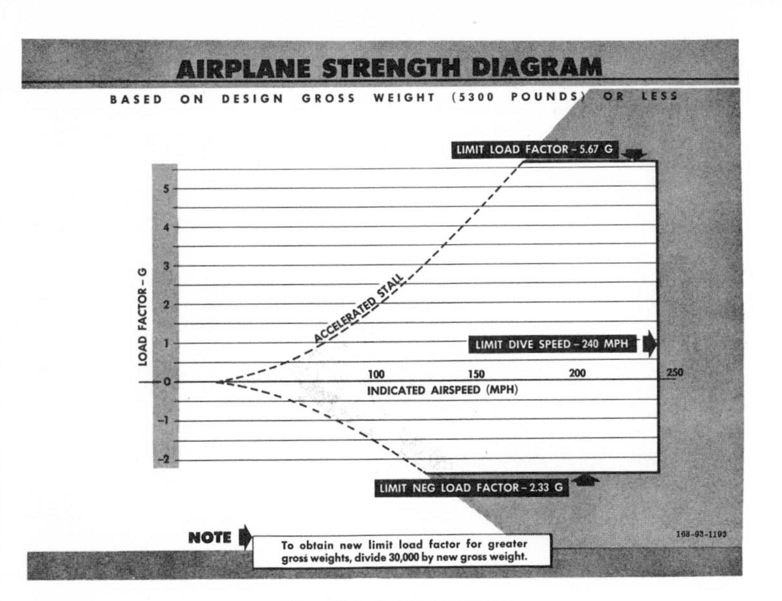

Figure 5-2. Airplane Strength Diagram

FLIGHT CHARACTERISTICS

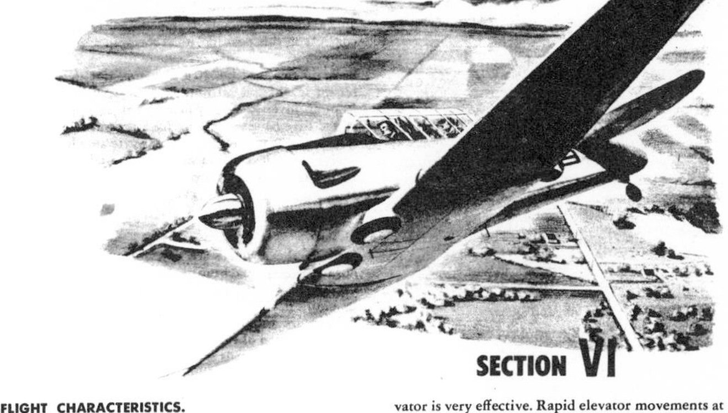

FLIGHT CHARACTERISTICS.

The airplane has good stability and control characteristics and when properly trimmed will tend to maintain level flight.

MANEUVERING FLIGHT.

Rapid airplane response to flight control movement during the normal speed range provides good acrobatic characteristics in this airplane. However, elevator stick forces in turns and pull-outs are purposely higher than elevator stick forces in fighter-type airplanes. This feature is to help you prevent imposing an excessive G-load on the airplane during acrobatics.

CAUTION

Do not trim the airplane during any acrobatic maneuvers in an attempt to reduce stick forces, as only small elevator stick forces are then required to exceed the structural limits for the airplane.

FLIGHT CONTROLS.

All flight controls are very effective throughout the normal speed range, and only moderate stick movement is required to maneuver the airplane. At high speeds, the airplane response to control movement is greater than at cruise speeds and abrupt movement of the controls must be avoided to prevent exceeding the G limit of the airplane. Near stalling speeds, the ailerons are least effective, the rudder is fairly effective, and the elevator is very effective. Rapid elevator movements at low speed should be avoided to prevent an inadvertent stall. Elevator and rudder trim tab adjustments are sufficient to trim elevator stick forces and rudder pedal forces to zero throughout the normal speed range. Right rudder pedal force may be required during low-speed full-power conditions. The aileron trim tab is not adjustable from the cockpit.

FLIGHT WITH EXTERNAL LOADS.

Flight characteristics of the airplane with external loads are similar to those encountered with the clean airplane.

SPINS.

The airplane spin characteristics are illustrated in figure 6-1. The spin characteristics remain essentially the same whether the gear and flaps are up or down or whether the spin is to the left or the right. Some slight difference in the magnitude of the oscillations and canopy vibration may be noted. Normal spin entry is accomplished in the conventional manner by application of full rudder in the desired direction at point of stall and simultaneous application of full back stick with ailerons neutral. These control positions must be held with the spin until the desired number of turns has been completed. The minimum altitude for intentionally entering a spin is 10,000 feet above the terrain. (Inverted spins are prohibited.)

SPIN RECOVERY.

Recovery from normal or inverted spins is effected by vigorous application of full opposite rudder followed by stick movement (slightly forward of neutral for normal spins and slightly aft of neutral for inverted spins). Leave ailerons neutral. Immediately following application of recovery controls, the nose of the airplane will drop and the spin will accelerate rapidly for approximately one-half to three-fourths turn. Hold the controls in this position until the spin stops; then immediately relax rudder pressure to neutral. Slowly apply back pressure on the stick to round out the dive and regain level-flight attitude. During the final recovery from an inverted spin, you may half-roll from the inverted dive before applying back pressure on the stick to round out the dive. Move throttle slowly to cruise setting after level-flight attitude is attained. Elevator stick forces during recovery will be lighter if the elevator trim adjustment is maintained for the level-flight cruise condition.

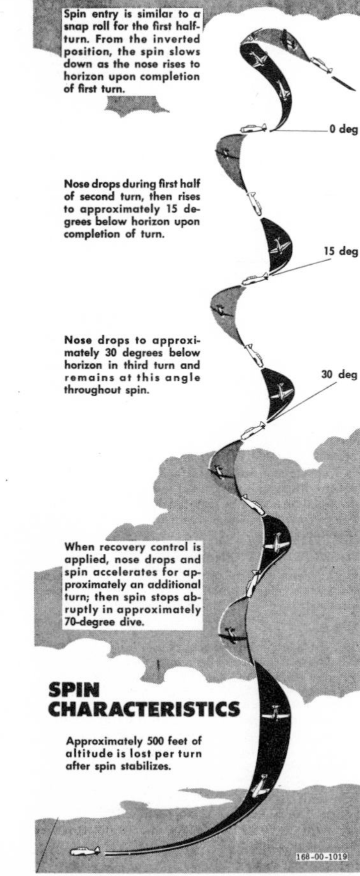

Figure 6-1. Spin Characteristics

STALLS.

Stalls in this airplane are not violent. You can feel a normal stall approaching as the controls begin to loosen up and the airplane develops a sinking "mushy" feeling. In addition, you can see the stalling attitude. When the stall occurs, there is a slight buffeting of the elevator and a vibration of the fuselage, and the nose or a wing drops. Stalling speeds with gear and flaps up or down—power on or off—with different gross weights at varying degrees of bank are given in figure 6-3. Conditions that affect stalling speeds and characteristics are shown in figure 6-2.

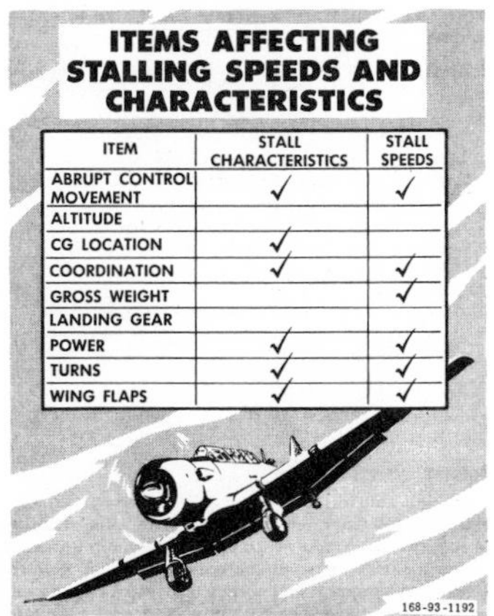

ITEMS AFFECTING STALLING SPEEDS AND CHARACTERISTICS

ITEM	STALL CHARACTERISTICS	STALL SPEEDS
ABRUPT CONTROL MOVEMENT	✓	✓
ALTITUDE		
CG LOCATION	✓	
COORDINATION	✓	✓
GROSS WEIGHT		✓
LANDING GEAR		
POWER	✓	✓
TURNS	✓	✓
WING FLAPS	✓	✓

Figure 6-2. Items Affecting Stalling Speeds and Characteristics

STALL RECOVERY.

The importance of proper stall recovery technique cannot be stressed too much. Because the elevator is very effective at stalling speeds, recovery is quick and positive. However, rough elevator use or failure to regain sufficient flying speed following a normal stall can cause an accelerated or high-speed stall. You can recover from partial stalls by reducing back pressure on the stick or by adding sufficient power to maintain control of the airplane. The standard procedure for recovering from a stall is as follows:

1. Move stick forward quickly and smoothly. Avoid jamming or snapping the stick forward abruptly, to prevent an undesirable nose-low attitude and momentary engine stoppage.

2. At the same time, advance the throttle in a smooth movement to the sea-level stop.

Note

Be sure to move the stick and throttle together smoothly. Do not allow the nose to drop too far below the horizon.

3. If a wing drops, apply opposite rudder at the first indication.

4. Use aileron as soon as it becomes effective, in order to reduce slipping and skidding as much as possible. After the nose has been lowered, speed will increase rapidly.

5. When you attain safe flying speed, raise the nose to level flight with steady back pressure on the stick. Avoid abrupt changes of attitude.

6. Retard throttle to cruising power after leveling off.

Enter all stalls at a safe altitude above the ground. Recoveries should be completed at 4000 feet or higher above the terrain. Remember that considerable altitude can be lost in a stall maneuver.

INDICATED STALLING SPEEDS—MPH

POWER ON STALLING SPEEDS ARE BASED ON ESTIMATED DATA

GROSS WEIGHT LB	GEAR AND FLAPS UP						GEAR AND FLAPS DOWN					
	POWER ON (MAX CONTINUOUS POWER)			POWER OFF (WINDMILLING PROP)			POWER ON (APPROACH POWER)			POWER OFF (WINDMILLING PROP)		
	Level	30 Bank	45 Bank	Level	30 Bank	45 Bank	Level	30 Bank	45 Bank	Level	30 Bank	45 Bank
6000	72	78	88	78	84	92	63	70	79	67	72	81
5500	67	74	84	75	80	89	60	66	75	63	69	77
5000	61	70	79	71	76	84	55	62	71	59	65	73
4500	54	64	74	66	72	80	51	57	66	55	61	69

168-93-1179

Figure 6-3. Stalling Speeds

PRACTICE STALLS.

The following practice maneuvers will acquaint you with the stall traits and speed of the airplane under various flight conditions. For both power-on and power-off stalls, set the propeller control to obtain 1850 rpm. This setting will prevent engine limitations from being exceeded inadvertently during recovery. Retard the throttle smoothly for power-off stall; set manifold pressure at 25 inches for power-on stalls. Canopies should be closed during practice stalls to prevent exhaust flame from entering cockpit in case of backfire.

PRACTICE STALL—GEAR AND FLAPS DOWN, POWER OFF, STRAIGHT AHEAD. Set propeller control for 1850 rpm and mixture control for smooth operation. Close the throttle and maintain altitude. When airspeed approaches approximately 110 mph, lower full flaps. Establish a 90 mph glide and trim the airplane. Pull the nose up to a three-point attitude and hold until the stall occurs. Observe the qualities of the airplane in the stall. Note the *feel*. After the airplane breaks to the right or left, or stalls straight ahead, perform a standard stall recovery as the nose passes through the horizon. Raise the landing gear and raise the flaps in slow stages as soon as possible. Retard the throttle to 25 inches manifold pressure.

PRACTICE STALL—GEAR AND FLAPS UP, POWER ON, STRAIGHT AHEAD. Raise nose to approximately 40 degrees above the horizon. Hold this attitude with wings level and nose steady. As the stall approaches, observe the looseness of the controls, attitude of the airplane, and the tone of the engine. Notice how the airplane shudders when the stall occurs. As the stall occurs, apply brisk forward pressure to the stick and, at the same time, advance the throttle to the sea-level stop. First use rudder to pick up the low wing; then blend in aileron as it becomes effective with the increase in airspeed. When flying speed is reached, ease airplane out of dive and back to cruising attitude, and reduce throttle to 25 inches manifold pressure.

PRACTICE STALL—GEAR AND FLAPS UP, POWER ON, 20-DEGREE BANK. Enter a coordinated climbing turn with a bank of approximately 20 degrees. Raise the nose approximately 40 degrees above the horizon. Keep the nose turning at a steady rate until the stall occurs. When the stall occurs, apply brisk forward pressure to the stick and advance the throttle to the sea-level stop. When you have enough flying speed to make ailerons effective, make a coordinated roll out of the turn and dive. Return to level flight as in straight-ahead stalls. Reduce throttle to 25 inches manifold pressure.

PRACTICE STALL—GEAR DOWN, FLAPS UP, POWER OFF, STRAIGHT AHEAD. Close throttle completely, reduce airspeed to 100 mph IAS, and establish a normal glide. Retrim. Raise the nose to a landing attitude and hold it on a point straight ahead until the stall occurs. As you approach the stall, observe the looseness of controls, the "mushy" feeling of the airplane, and the dwindling airspeed. Remember, this is like a landing stall. Use standard recovery procedure. Reduce throttle to 25 inches manifold pressure and raise the landing gear.

PRACTICE STALL—GEAR DOWN, FLAPS UP, POWER OFF, 40-DEGREE BANK. This maneuver will help you recognize the stalls which may occur in power-off turns in traffic or landings. Assume a normal glide of 100 mph; then roll into a medium gliding turn with about 40 degrees of bank. Maintain a steady turn, raising the nose slightly until it is just above the horizon. It is necessary to increase back pressure on the stick to hold this attitude until the stall occurs. Make a standard recovery. After recovering speed, use coordinated controls to level the airplane. Reduce the throttle to 25 inches manifold pressure and raise the landing gear.

DIVES.

The handling characteristics in dives to the limit airspeed are good. All control movement is easy and effective, and the airplane responds rapidly. If you trim the airplane for level flight at Maximum Continuous Power, the tab settings will be satisfactory for diving, although some adjustment of rudder tab may be desired during the dive so that you will not have to hold rudder. The amount of forward stick pressure required to hold the airplane in a dive is relatively small, as is the amount of aileron pressure needed to keep the wings level. To determine the altitude lost in a constant 4 G pull-out dive recovery, see figure 6-4. Prior to entering a dive, close the canopy, and, to prevent excessive oil cooling, adjust oil cooler shutter control as necessary. Decrease rpm as necessary during the dive to prevent exceeding maximum engine overspeed.

At completion of dive, open throttle slowly to prevent partly cooled engine from cutting out.

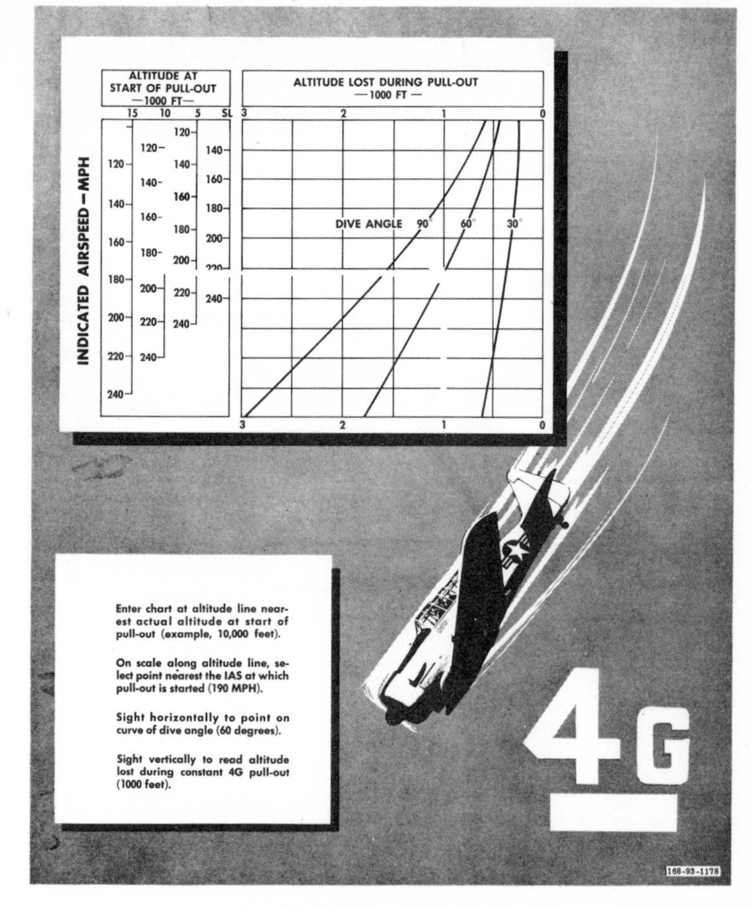

Figure 6-4. Altitude Loss in Dive Recovery—4G

SYSTEMS OPERATION

ENGINE.

USE OF TAKE-OFF (MILITARY) POWER.

It is often asked what the consequences would be if the 5-minute limit at Take-off Power were exceeded. Another frequent inquiry is how long a period must be allowed after the specified time limit has elapsed until Take-off Power can again be used. These questions are difficult to answer, since the time limit specified does not mean that engine damage will occur if the limits are exceeded, but is meant more to keep to a reasonable minimum the total operating time at high power, in the interest of prolonging engine life.

It is generally accepted that high-power operation of an engine results in increased wear and necessitates more frequent overhaul than low-power operation. However, it is apparent that a certain percentage of operating time must be at full power. The engine manufacturer allows for this in qualification tests in which much of the running is done at Take-off Power to prove ability to withstand the resulting loads. It is established in these runs that the engine will handle sustained high power without damage. Nevertheless, it is still the aim of the manufacturer and to the best interest of the pilot to keep within reasonable values the amount of high-power time accumulated in the field. The most satisfactory method for accomplishing this is to establish time limits that will keep pilots constantly aware of the desire to hold high-power periods to the shortest period that the flight plan will allow, so that the total accumulated time and resulting wear can be kept to a minimum. How the time at high power is accumulated is of secondary importance; i.e., it is no worse from the standpoint of engine wear to operate at Take-off Power for one hour straight than it is to operate in twelve 5-minute stretches, provided engine temperatures and pressures are within limits. In fact, the former procedure may even be preferable, as it eliminates temperature cycles which also promote engine wear. Thus, if flight conditions occasionally require exceeding time limits, this should not cause concern so long as constant effort is made to *keep the over-all time at Take-off Power to the minimum practicable.*

Another factor to be remembered in operating engines at high power is that full Take-off Power is to be preferred over take-off rpm with reduced manifold pressure. This procedure results in less engine wear for two reasons. First, the higher resulting brake horsepower decreases the time required to obtain the objective of such high-power operation. At take-off, for example, the use of full power decreases the time required to reach an altitude and airspeed where it is safe to reduce power, and shortens the time required to reach the airspeed that will provide more favorable cylinder cooling. Second, high rpm results in high loads on the reciprocating parts due to inertia forces. As these loads are partially offset by the gas pressure in the cylinder, the higher cylinder pressures resulting from use of full take-off manifold pressure will give lower net loads and less wear. Sustained high rpm is a major factor producing engine wear. It requires more "rpm minutes" and "piston ring miles" to take off with reduced manifold pressure. In addition to the engine wear factor, a take-off at reduced power is comparable to starting with approximately one-third of the runway behind the airplane. Therefore, full power should *always* be used on all take-offs.

MANUAL LEANING.

An important factor affecting engine power output is the fuel-air ratio of the inlet charge going to the cylinders. Since air density decreases with altitude, the mixture control must be manually adjusted to maintain a proper mixture. However, lean mixtures must be avoided, especially when the engine is operating near its maximum output. It is well to closely observe the cylinder head temperature whenever lean mixtures are used. If the mixture is too lean, one or more of the following operational difficulties may result: rough engine operation, backfiring, overheating, detonation, sudden engine failure, or appreciable loss in engine power. Adjusting the mixture for smooth operation is accomplished by slowly pulling the mixture control toward LEAN until the engine definitely falters; immediately push the control slightly forward until the engine is again running smoothly. Then slowly push the control approximately 1/16 inch toward RICH.

THROTTLE "JOCKEYING."

Since there is no advantage to "jockeying" the throttle, and because it can result in damage to the engine, it should be avoided. "Jockeying" the throttle when the engine is cold frequently causes backfire with accompanying fire hazard. When the engine is hot, "jockeying" the throttle will tend to "load up" and possibly choke the engine.

CHANGING ENGINE POWER SETTINGS.

One of the basic limitations placed on engine operation is imposed by the amount of pressure developed in the cylinders during combustion. If this pressure becomes excessive, it can cause detonation and will result in eventual engine failure. Since improper coordination in the use of the throttle and propeller control can cause these limitations to be exceeded, it is important to learn the correct sequence in which these controls should be used. *Whenever the engine power is to be reduced, retard the throttle first—then retard the propeller control. Conversely, when increasing engine power, advance the propeller control first—then advance the throttle.*

CARBURETOR ICING

A characteristic of carburetor icing is that ice will form more readily when the *mixture* temperature in the carburetor is between −10°C and +3°C. Carburetor icing usually occurs during times when the *free air* temperature is about +4°C to +8°C. Ice will also form more readily when the engine is operated under a low-power cruise condition; therefore, a higher power setting should be selected when icing conditions are prevalent. The formation of ice can be detected by a gradual decrease of manifold pressure, but rpm will remain constant, as the propeller governor will automatically maintain the existing rpm setting. Moving the carburetor air control to HOT will eliminate the ice in the carburetor, and the manifold pressure will return to almost the original setting. During operation in cold, clear, nonicing air where cylinder head and carburetor mixture temperatures drop to values sufficiently low to cause rough engine operation, carburetor heat should be increased just enough to eliminate the roughness.

DETONATION.

Detonation is the result of one type of abnormal combustion of part of the fuel-air mixture. The other prevalent form of abnormal combustion is preignition. When detonation occurs, combustion is normal until approximately 80 percent of the charge is burning. At that point, the rate of combustion speeds up tremendously, resulting in an explosion or nearly instantaneous combustion. This explosion actually pounds the cylinder walls, producing "knock." This "knock," or pounding of the cylinder walls, can cause an engine failure. In an airplane, the "knock" is not heard because of other engine and propeller noises. However, detonation can be detected by observing the exhaust for visible puffs of black smoke, glowing carbon particles, or a small, sharp, whitish-orange flame. In addition, a rapid increase in cylinder head temperatures often indicates detonation. When detonation is evident, throttle reduction is the most immediate and surest remedy. *When detonation occurs, power is lost.* Contributing causes of detonation are as follows:

1. Low-octane fuel.

2. High cylinder head temperature caused by too long a climb at too low an airspeed or by too lean a mixture.

3. High mixture temperature caused by use of carburetor heat or by high outside air temperature.

4. Too high manifold pressure with other conditions favorable to detonation.

5. Improper mixture caused by faulty carburetor or too lean a mixture.

PREIGNITION.

Preignition is closely related to detonation. In fact, detonation often progresses into preignition. When the engine gets too hot, the mixture is ignited before the spark occurs. When this happens, much of the power is wasted trying to push the piston down while it is still rising in the cylinder. The power impulses are uneven, horsepower falls off, and the engine can be damaged from excessive pressures and temperatures. Preignition may be detected by backfiring through the carburetor and possibly by a rapid increase in cylinder head temperatures. When preignition is encountered, the throttle setting should be reduced immediately.

FUEL SYSTEM FLIGHT OPERATION.

During flight, the fuel selector should be moved alternately between 35.2 GAL. LEFT and 35.2 GAL. RIGHT to

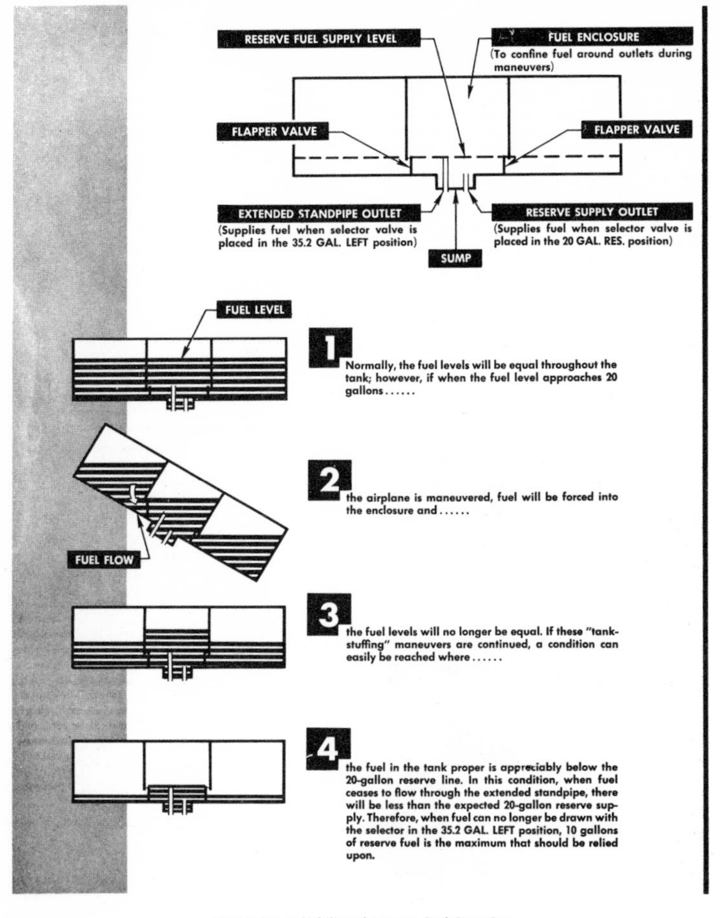

Figure 7-1. Reliability of Reserve Fuel Quantity

Since the engine is shut down with propeller at ***DECREASE*** rpm, it must be started at ***DECREASE*** rpm to ensure proper engine lubrication during starting.

OIL PRESSURE FROM PROPELLER GOVERNOR

OIL RETURN TO PROPELLER GOVERNOR

LOW PITCH (INCREASE RPM), PISTON FORCED OUT BY OIL PRESSURE

HIGH PITCH (DECREASE RPM), PISTON FORCED IN BY COUNTERWEIGHTS

168-44-260A

Figure 7-2. Propeller Operation

keep the fuel level in the wing tanks within 10 gallons of each other. When flying below 3000 feet above the ground, it is advisable to use 20 GAL. RES. or 55.2 GAL. RIGHT as a safety precaution to prevent inadvertent fuel starvation. Maneuvering flight, under certain conditions (figure 7-1), can cause a reduction in the available reserve to an amount as low as 10 gallons.

PROPELLER OPERATION.

The relationship between propeller pitch (blade angle), counterweight and propeller piston position, and function of engine oil pressure is schematically shown on figure 7-2. The engine speed is maintained constant by a governor which regulates the flow of engine oil to or from a piston incorporated in the propeller hub. A counterweight at the shank of each blade provides a force (proportionate to rpm) in opposition to engine oil pressure to effect a balance. The resultant action of the piston varies the propeller blade angle or pitch, thereby maintaining a constant engine rpm. The engine is shut down with the propeller at decrease rpm (high pitch) so that the oil in the hub piston will be returned to the oil tank. Therefore, the propeller control must be at DECREASE rpm when the engine is again started; otherwise, the immediate demand for oil to change the propeller pitch will decrease the available oil pressure necessary for engine lubrication during the start.

Section VIII
CREW DUTIES

Not applicable to this airplane.

ALL-WEATHER OPERATION

SECTION IX

Except for some repetition necessary for emphasis or continuity of thought, this section contains only those procedures that differ from, or are in addition to, the normal operating instructions contained in Section II.

NIGHT FLYING

There are no predominate differences between night flying procedures and day flying procedures. Exhaust glare will obviously be more pronounced during night flights, however, but should be no cause for alarm. Refer to Section II for night flight interior check, take-off, and landing procedures.

INSTRUMENT FLIGHT PROCEDURES

Stability and rapid acceleration or deceleration are the outstanding instrument flight characteristics of the airplane. All the necessary flight instruments are provided. In an emergency, flight on the basic flight instruments (turn-and-bank indicator and airspeed indicator) can be safely accomplished. Radio compass, range reception, vhf transmission, and vhf reception are all provided in addition to interphone communication between cockpits. Remember, since power settings are somewhat higher during certain phases of instrument flight, the airplane range will be slightly decreased.

Note

All turns are single-needle-width standard-rate (3 degrees per second) turns.

PRIOR TO TAKE-OFF.

1. Check G file for inclusion of AN 08-15-1 (Radio Facilities Charts), AN 08-15-2 (USAF Radio Data and Flight Information), and Pilot's Handbooks—Continental United States.

2. Check suction gage for proper indication.

3. Check that the pitot head cover has been removed. Turn pitot heater on and have outside observer verify its operation. Turn pitot heater off until just prior to take-off.

4. Check airspeed indicator needle at zero. Check airspeed correction card for any deviation at the speed range to be flown.

5. If the directional gyro has been actuated for at least 5 minutes, the rotor will have attained proper operating speed. Cage the gyro and then, while turning the knob, uncage it. The dial card should revolve with the knob when the gyro is caged, but not when the gyro is uncaged. Set the directional gyro so that it corresponds to the reading of the magnetic compass.

6. If the gyro horizon has been actuated for at least 5 minutes, the rotor will have attained proper operating speed. Cage the instrument and then uncage it. After the instrument is uncaged, the horizon bar should return to the correct position for the attitude of the airplane. Temporary vibration of the horizon bar is permissible.

Note

If the horizon bar temporarily departs from horizontal position while the airplane is being taxied straight ahead, or if the bar tips more than 5 degrees during taxiing turns, the instrument is not operating properly.

7. Obtain station altimeter setting (sea-level barometric pressure) from control tower operator. When the altimeter is set, the pointers should indicate local field elevation. If the altimeter registers within 75 feet, it may be used, provided the error is properly considered when the instrument is reset during flight.

8. Check operation of turn-and-bank indicator by observing proper response of needle and ball when turns are made during taxiing.

9. Check rate-of-climb indicator needle at zero.

Note

If the needle does not indicate zero, tap the instrument panel. If it still indicates incorrectly, readjust it by use of the screw in the lower left corner of the instrument.

10. Check accuracy of the magnetic compass by comparing its reading to the published runway heading.

11. Check that clock is operating and set to correct time.

12. Move the carburetor heat control handle to HOT. Proper operation is verified by a resultant drop in manifold pressure as the mixture temperature increases. Return carburetor heat control handle to COLD.

13. Check instruments for readings within proper ranges.

14. Check operation of all radio equipment. Adjust tuning as desired.

INSTRUMENT TAKE-OFF.

Preparation, power settings, and take-off and climb speeds are identical to those used in normal take-off. Since use of flaps reduces rate of climb, they should not be used for instrument take-offs.

1. When cleared for take-off, taxi to the center of the runway and align the airplane, as nearly as possible, straight down the centerline of the runway. Hold the airplane with the brakes. Set directional gyro to the published runway heading.

2. When ready, advance throttle to obtain 1000 to 1200 rpm. Release brakes and, as the airplane starts to roll, advance throttle smoothly to the sea-level stop.

3. Maintain directional control by reference to directional gyro. When elevator control becomes effective, raise the tail slightly and allow the airplane to leave the ground with the nose slightly lower than in a three-point attitude, as indicated on the gyro horizon.

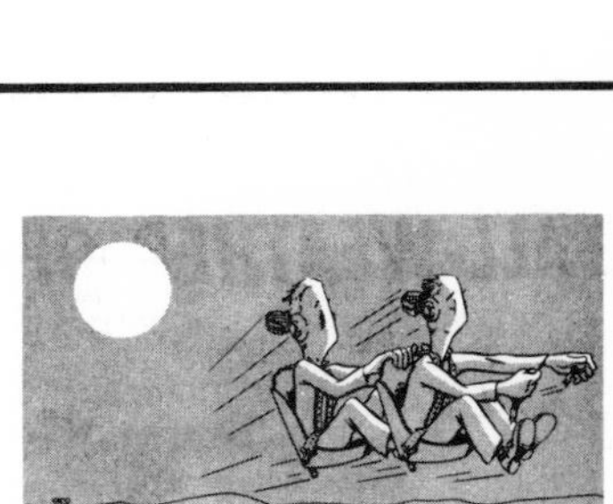

Prior to take-off under instrument conditions, special attention should be given to gyro instruments and airplane trim. Any irregularity could have serious consequences.

4. Hold this pitch attitude and, as the airplane breaks ground, hold the wings level by reference to the gyro horizon. Hold direction by reference to the directional gyro.

5. As soon as the altimeter and rate-of-climb indicator begin to register a climb, retract the landing gear.

6. Reduce the throttle setting and propeller control setting to give approximately 30 in. Hg manifold pressure and 2000 rpm.

INSTRUMENT CLIMB.

1. Establish a rate of climb to obtain approximately 500 feet per minute on the rate-of-climb indicator until normal climbing speed is reached; then trim airplane to maintain this airspeed.

2. Leave traffic and climb to assigned flight altitude in accordance with local air traffic regulations. Do not exceed a 30-degree bank during climbing turns.

INSTRUMENT CRUISING FLIGHT.

Since trim of the airplane will change rapidly when increasing or decreasing speed, adjustment of the trim tabs will be necessary until speed is stabilized. Since no aileron trim facilities are provided, balance the airplane laterally by maintaining an even fuel level. While *changing* cruising airspeed, momentarily overpower or underpower (3 to 5 in. Hg) beyond the desired power setting for a quicker response. The recommended airspeeds, shown in the following chart, will provide a safe margin above stall and good controllability for practice instrument flight. The following power settings will normally give the standard airspeeds listed.

Note

If landing gear is extended, the power settings should be slightly higher.

RECOMMENDED AIRSPEEDS	RPM	APPROX MAN. PRESS. (In. Hg)	MIXTURE
Climb to cruising altitude—110 mph IAS	2000	30	Mixture adjusted for smoothest operation above 3000 feet.
Slow cruise—110 mph IAS	1850	18	
Normal cruise—130 mph IAS	1850	21	
Fast cruise—140 mph IAS	1850	24	
Climb—500 fpm—110 mph IAS	1850	25	
Descent—500 fpm—110 mph IAS	1850	13	
GCA airspeed—20-degree flaps—100 mph IAS	2000	16-18	RICH

DESCENT.

Normal descent procedures are followed.

HOLDING.

If holding for an extended period is necessary, fuel can be conserved by using a power setting of 1600 rpm and enough manifold pressure to maintain an airspeed of 100 mph IAS.

INSTRUMENT APPROACHES.

Radio range letdown and low-visibility approaches are standard.

GROUND CONTROLLED APPROACH. Procedure for landing under instrument conditions by use of directions from ground controlled approach radar equipment after letdown on a radio range is as follows:

1. Establish contact with GCA over GCA pickup point.

2. Hold 110 mph IAS until final turn is completed, running through GCA prelanding cockpit check as instructed by the GCA controller.

3. After completing turn to final approach and prior to intercepting the glide path, lower flaps 20 degrees.

4. As glide path is intercepted, reduce throttle setting to obtain 17 in. Hg manifold pressure and descend as directed by the GCA final controller.

ICE AND RAIN.

During a winter fog or rain, watch for icing on wings from propeller blast during engine run-up. Don't take off in sleet if you can avoid it because it may freeze on the wings before you can gain altitude. If carburetor ice has formed during ground operation, use carburetor heat to remove ice prior to take-off and as necessary during take-off.

The carburetor is susceptible to icing and may ice up at any time under actual instrument flight conditions. Except in extreme cases, carburetor mixture temperatures of approximately 3°C will be sufficient to clear the carburetor or prevent icing.

Engine roughness and a slight drop in manifold pressure are indications of ice forming in the carburetor. If carburetor icing is indicated, carburetor heat should first be applied at a somewhat higher temperature than is normally used and then readjusted as necessary to prevent further icing. Fuel consumption will increase slightly with the application of carburetor heat. If icing is encountered during low rpm operation, increase the engine speed and manifold pressure and enrich the mixture.

If ice has accumulated on wings, make wide, shallow turns at a speed greater than normal, especially during the approach. Use flaps with care. Remember, stalling speed increases with ice. The only units that incorporate provisions to prevent icing are the pitot head and carburetor. Additional information concerning carburetor icing is given in Section VII.

FLIGHT IN TURBULENCE AND THUNDERSTORMS.

A pilot, using modern equipment and possessing a combination of proper experience, common sense, and instrument flying proficiency, can safely fly thunderstorms. However, flight through a thunderstorm should be avoided if it is at all possible.

Since circumstances may force you at some time to enter a zone of severe turbulence, you should be familiar with the techniques recommended for flying this airplane under such circumstances. Power setting and pitch attitude are the keys to proper flight technique in turbulent air. The power setting and pitch attitude for the desired penetration airspeed should be established before entrance into the storm and, if maintained throughout the storm, should result in a constant airspeed regardless of any false indications by the airspeed indicator. Instructions for preparing to enter a storm and flying in it are given in the following paragraphs.

BEFORE TAKE-OFF. Perform the following checks before take-off when flight through a storm is anticipated:

1. Check turbulent air penetration speed chart (figure 9-1) for best penetration speed.

2. Make a thorough analysis of the general weather to determine thunderstorm areas, and prepare a flight

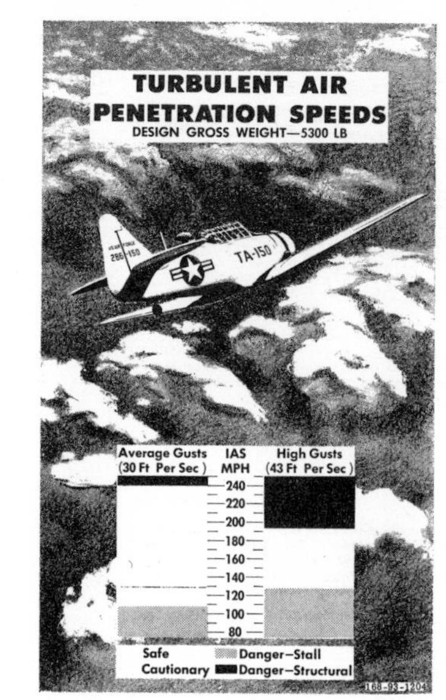

Figure 9-1. Turbulent Air Penetration Speeds

plan that will avoid thunderstorm areas whenever possible.

3. Be sure to check proper operation of all flight instruments, navigation equipment, pitot heater, carburetor air heater, and panel lights before attempting flight through thunderstorm areas.

APPROACHING THE STORM. It is imperative that you prepare the airplane prior to entering a zone of turbulent air. If the storm cannot be seen, its proximity can be detected by radio crash static. Prepare the airplane as follows:

1. Accurately fix position prior to actual entry into thunderstorm area.

2. Propeller control set to obtain 1900 rpm for gyroscopic stability.

3. Mixture control adjusted for smooth engine operation.

4. Pitot heater switch ON.

5. Carburetor air control adjusted as required.

6. Throttle adjusted as necessary to obtain desired penetration speed.

7. Check suction gage for proper reading and gyro instruments for correct settings.

8. Tighten safety belt. Lock shoulder harness.

9. Turn off any radio equipment rendered useless by static.

10. To minimize blinding effect of lightning at night, turn cockpit lights full bright or use dark glasses, adjust seat low, and don't stare outside airplane.

When flying through turbulent air, do not lower gear and flaps, as they decrease the aerodynamic efficiency of the airplane.

IN THE STORM. While flying through the storm, observe the following precautions:

1. Maintain, throughout the storm, the power setting and pitch attitude established before entering the storm. Hold these constant and your airspeed will be constant, regardless of the airspeed indicator.

2. Maintain attitude. Concentrate principally on holding a level attitude by reference to the gyro horizon.

3. Maintain original heading. Do not make any turns unless absolutely necessary.

4. Don't chase the airspeed indicator, since doing so will result in extreme airplane attitudes. If a sudden gust should be encountered while the airplane is in a nose-high attitude, a stall might easily result. Because of rapid changes in vertical gust velocity or rain clogging the pitot tube, the airspeed may momentarily fluctuate as much as 70 mph.

5. Use as little elevator control as possible to maintain your attitude in order to minimize the stresses imposed on the airplane.

6. The altimeter and rate-of-climb indicator may be unreliable in thunderstorms because of differential barometric pressure within the storm. A gain or loss of several thousand feet may be expected. Altitude must be allowed to vary, to let the airplane ride out the storm. Make allowance for this condition in determining a minimum safe altitude.

Note

Normally, the least turbulent area in a thunderstorm will be at altitudes between 6000 and 8000 feet above the terrain. Altitudes between 10,000 and 20,000 feet are usually the most turbulent.

7. Maintain a constant power setting and pitch attitude unless airspeed falls off to 60 percent above power-on stalling speed, or unless airspeed increases to approximately 30 percent above maximum penetration airspeed.

COLD-WEATHER PROCEDURES

The success of low-temperature operation depends greatly on the preparation made previously during engine shutdown and postflight procedures as outlined in the following paragraphs. Icing conditions, however, are covered in the instructions for instrument flight.

BEFORE ENTERING THE AIRPLANE.

1. Have "Y" drain and oil tank sump checked for free flow. If no oil flow is obtained, heat should be applied.

Note

If oil was not diluted when the engine was previously shut down, heating will be necessary at temperatures below 2°C (35°F). At temperatures below −18°C (0°F), heat should be applied to the engine and accessories. Below −30°C (−22°F), it may be necessary to apply heat also to the battery, cockpits, master brake cylinder, and actuating cylinders.

2. Have moisture drained from all fuel tanks and fuel system sumps; if they are frozen, heat should be applied first. Check fuel and oil tank vent lines for free passage.

3. Check gear and shock struts free of dirt and ice.

4. Have protective covers removed from airplane and any snow or ice removed from surfaces, control hinges, propeller, pitot tube, fuel and oil vents, and crankcase breather outlet.

5. Check freedom of propeller periodically to determine engine stiffness. If propeller cannot be moved easily, continue preheat.

6. Have engine cover and ground heater removed.

BEFORE STARTING ENGINE.

1. Have external power source connected, to conserve battery life for use during in-flight emergencies.

2. Have oil immersion heater removed.

3. Have propeller pulled through at least two revolutions.

4. Prime engine four to six strokes.

Note

Rapid priming action may be necessary to vaporize the fuel sufficiently.

STARTING ENGINE.

1. After engine starts, continue priming until engine is running smoothly.

2. If there is no indication of oil pressure after 30 seconds running, or if pressure drops after a few minutes of ground operation, stop engine and investigate.

3. Use carburetor heat to assist fuel vaporization.

WARM-UP AND GROUND TESTS.

1. Check all instruments for normal operation.

2. When oil temperature and pressure are normal, advance the throttle to 1400 rpm, and pull propeller control to full DECREASE position until a drop of 200 rpm is obtained; then return control to full INCREASE position. Repeat procedure three times to ensure that hot oil is in propeller dome.

3. Operate wing flaps through at least one complete cycle.

4. Perform all ground tests requiring electrical power before disconnecting external power source.

Note

The battery cannot carry the electrical load imposed by ground operation of pitot heater and radios. Minimize load on the electrical system until the generator "cuts in."

5. Have external power source disconnected and turn battery-disconnect switch ON.

TAXIING INSTRUCTIONS.

Use only essential electrical equipment to conserve battery life while taxiing at low engine speeds. Avoid slushy and icy areas. Apply brakes cautiously to prevent skidding. Avoid taxiing in deep snow, as steering and taxiing are extremely difficult and frozen brakes are likely to result.

BEFORE TAKE-OFF.

1. Check controls very carefully for free and proper movement.

2. Hold brakes and run up engine to 2000 rpm until spark plugs have burned clean and engine is operating smoothly. Then check magnetos.

3. Apply carburetor heat as necessary to maintain carburetor mixture temperature within limits during take-off.

4. Place pitot heat switch ON just before rolling into position for take-off.

TAKE-OFF.

At start of take-off run, advance throttle rapidly to take-off setting and check that full power is available. If full power is not obtained, immediately discontinue take-off. Since cold, dry air has a greater density, engine power output and airplane lift are increased.

AFTER TAKE-OFF.

After take-off from a wet snow- or slush-covered field, operate the landing gear and flaps through several complete cycles to prevent their freezing in the retracted position. Expect considerable slower operation of the landing gear and flaps in cold weather.

CLIMB.

1. Adjust carburetor air control as necessary to prevent carburetor icing.

2. Adjust oil cooler shutter control as necessary to maintain correct oil temperature.

DURING FLIGHT.

1. At low outside air temperatures, especially during low-power cruising operation, the fuel-air mixture ratio may be too cold for proper vaporization and fuel economy. Use carburetor heat as necessary to obtain smooth engine operation and to eliminate plug fouling.

2. Operate propeller control every 30 minutes, obtaining approximately a 300 rpm increase and decrease from cruising position; then return to cruise rpm.

3. Adjust cockpit heat as necessary.

DESCENT.

1. Use power during the descent to prevent engine from being cooled too rapidly.

2. Increase carburetor heat as necessary.

3. Mixture control RICH.

APPROACH.

1. Make a longer, lower approach than normal so that some power is needed to reach the runway. Use carburetor heat.

2. Pump brake pedals several times.

LANDING.

Use normal landing procedure.

STOPPING ENGINE.

OIL DILUTION. Before shutdown, the engine oil should be diluted unless the entire oil system is to be drained. If it is necessary to service the oil tank, shut down the engine and have it serviced before diluting. Then restart the engine and dilute as follows:

1. Run engine at 1000 rpm.

2. During dilution, maintain oil temperature from 5°C to 50°C and oil pressure above 15 psi. Reset throttle, if necessary, to maintain these conditions. If oil temperature is above 50°C, shut down engine and allow oil to cool below 40°C; then restart and dilute.

3. Hold oil dilution switch ON, as required by lowest expected temperature, for time indicated in the following table:

ANTICIPATED TEMPERATURE	TIME—MINUTES
4°C to −12°C (40°F to 10°F)	3
−12°C to −29°C (10°F to −20°F)	6
−29°C to −46°C (−20°F to −50°F)	9

[Add one minute of dilution for each further drop of 5°C (9°F) below − 46°C.]

4. Dilute the oil in the propeller by operating the propeller control during the latter part of the dilution time interval. Advance throttle to 1400 rpm and move propeller control back until a decrease of approximately 200 rpm is obtained; then return control to full INCREASE. Repeat operation three times.

BEFORE LEAVING THE AIRPLANE.

1. Release the brakes.

2. Check dirt and ice removed from shock struts.

3. Inspect oil and fuel tanks and engine breather to verify absence of any accumulated ice.

4. Leave canopy partially open to prevent cracking of transparent areas due to differential contraction. Air circulation also retards formation of frost.

5. Have protective covers installed.

6. Have oil tank sump, "Y" drain, and fuel sumps drained of condensation approximately 30 minutes after stopping the engine. If the airplane is to be idle for several days, the oil may be drained.

7. If specific gravity of battery is less than 1.250, have battery removed for service. If layover of several days is anticipated, or if temperature is below −29°C (−20°F) and airplane will be idle more than 4 hours, have the battery removed.

3064